UNDER THE
INFLUENCE

UNDER THE
INFLUENCE

California's Intoxicating
Spiritual and Cultural Impact on America

MONICA GANAS

BrazosPress
a division of Baker Publishing Group
Grand Rapids, Michigan

© 2010 by Monica Ganas

Published by Brazos Press
a division of Baker Publishing Group
P.O. Box 6287, Grand Rapids, MI 49516-6287
www.brazospress.com

Printed in the United States of America

Library of Congress Cataloging-in-Publication Data
Ganas, Monica, 1950–
    Under the influence : California's intoxicating spiritual and cultural impact on America / Monica Ganas.
        p.   cm.
    Includes bibliographical references.
    ISBN 978-1-58743-179-1 (pbk.)
    1. California—Civilization. 2. Popular culture—Moral and ethical aspects—California. 3. Religion and culture—California. I. Title.
F866.2.G36 2010
979.4—dc22   2010002027

10   11   12   13   14   15   16   7   6   5   4   3   2   1

To Scotty, Nick, Erin, and Dave,
my favorite Californians,
I love you

Contents

Acknowledgments

There's an African saying, "umuntu ngumuntu ngabantu," a person is a person because of other people. This book is a book for the same reason. To mention the names of everyone that helped me in some way would be to write another book. So I'll beg for grace in advance and will consider this a highlight reel of the countless favors done me, and my ongoing appreciation for them. I'll begin by thanking a prayer group to which I belong called the Niños, because I'm sure I would never have started this book, let alone finished it, without their prayerful encouragement and advice. Several in this group are faculty at my university, and my friend and colleague Joseph Bentz was the one who reminded me I was overdue for sabbatical and walked me through the steps to apply so I could begin this project. I am so grateful to Joe, to Diana Glyer, and to the other niños, I could weep.

I'm thankful for my mom's prayers and to my sister Enid for keeping my mom alive. I'm blessed with terrific family and friends, some lifelong ones, who spur me on continually; I'm thankful for and moved by the hospitality of my friends in Northern California during my research there. While on sabbatical, I stayed a month with my childhood friend Jan Pollard. Jan is the best writer I know, and she has been hugely influential in shaping whatever is best in my work. It's hard to imagine how I'd have gotten through the proposal for this book had I not been given the quiet, insistent space at her house to pound away at the draft she then edited. My friend Scott Young was kind enough to arrange for a meeting with Rodney Clapp of Brazos, who was kind enough to help me from the very beginning of this project and to encourage me throughout.

Azusa Pacific University is a fantastic place to work; so much so, my family teases me, that I never leave it. In addition to the semester sabbatical, APU has supported my work in numerous ways, including the award of a research grant. The writer of the grant proposal, Kevin Walker, is responsible for the first paragraph of this book, and his intelligence and eloquence are unmatched. Another brilliant colleague and friend, Craig Keen, has shared his outstanding research and insights in support of chapter 9 of this book, and I deeply appreciate his graciousness. My provost Michael Whyte, my dean David Weeks, Carole Lambert, Bev Stanford, Tom Andrews, Nancy Brashear, Elizabeth Gonzales, and so many others here have been helpful and kind beyond measure.

Then there are my students and alumni, who I suspect conspire to astonish me. Danielle Luchtenburg sacrificed hours and hours of time to the deadening job of formatting my documentation. I'll never find words enough to thank this dear and charming friend, whose generosity and work ethic are just plain inspirational. I thank my smart, perceptive research assistants Kerry Gallagher and Sarah Stanley, as well as Trina Merry, all of whom acted as important sounding boards in the early stages of this work, and made me laugh a lot when laughs were sorely needed. Kerry has remained a steady cheerleader, as has Mikael Taylor whose help with my considerable teaching duties has freed me up to make the final push this year to complete my writing.

My wonderful son, Nick, and son-in-law, David Gaw, are both alums of this university, and their stirring and meaningful remarks, Nicky's late-night talks, and Dave's ongoing help with technology have meant the world to me. But the alum to whom

I owe the most is unquestionably my daughter, Erin. Over the years, Erin has partnered with me in one insurmountable undertaking after another, both artistic and academic. She is the literal embodiment of encouragement, that is, she makes me brave. She is an extraordinary thinker whose insights sometimes make me (and others) gasp aloud, and looking over the pages of this book, I see her guidance everywhere. Her wit, compassion, and conviction bring to mind my husband, Scott.

There's a reason, I think, that writers seem prone to thank their spouses the most heartily. Beyond the patience they show with the long hours and occasional moodiness writing can represent, there's that distracted gaze writing creates, one that spouses can choose to ignore, choose to forgive, or, as in my lucky case, choose to engage. My husband talked me through one idea after another. He planned our entire vacation around my research, made all the arrangements, and traveled to all the museums, missions, institutes, you name it, with ongoing enthusiasm and indispensable input. Every time he saw the possibility of a lead, a document, or a roadside attraction I might have missed, a single sight or sound that might be valuable to me, he brought it to my attention. He read every chapter and cheered for it. He was nothing short of heroic. And, oh yeah, he coined the word "Cal-types."

I don't deserve the great goodness of the people I know, but at least I know enough to be very, very grateful; so with all my heart, thank you.

1

"Poppies, My Dear"

The Intoxicating Effect of California-ism

Abraham Lincoln once observed that the fate of the United States would rest on California. In an era preceding the mass culture unleashed by the electronic age, it would have been impossible for him to know the full scope of his prediction. At the time, Lincoln was referring to California's decision regarding slavery, since a "slave state" on the West Coast would mean a slave nation—a land void of any basis for liberty. The slavery issue was ultimately settled outside of California, by Lincoln's action in the Civil War. But his question set the precedent for California, a land that routinely raises the same kind of vital human questions and forcefully proposes specific answers for each new generation. California continually compels all Americans to decide exactly what our national character should be.

From its beginning, California has played a major role in determining American national identity through politics, economics, entertainment, social conventions, and even spirituality. What I'm suggesting now is that the sum of these factors in our own time culminates in an emergent cultural, philosophic, and sometimes pseudo-religious system that I call *California-ism*. Stephen Schwartz makes the point that California's "unique, phantasmagorical mentality has been a powerful force in the making of the American mind, flowing irresistibly from West to East." He concludes that "the amazing thing was how quickly America (and the world) surrendered to the Californian intoxication."[1] My question is, should Americans try to sleep off this intoxication?

The wicked witch in *The Wizard of Oz* cast her somnolent spell with the poppy, both a well-known opiate and the state flower of California. A narcotic is an apt emblem for the state since it is no secret that California has wielded a hypnotic effect on the icons and ideologies of our nation, and eventually those of many others. Sometimes I think the so-called California dream might more accurately be called a hallucination. This is the subject of the Red Hot Chili Peppers song, "Californication," and a television series by the same name explores the values, behaviors, and attitudes of the state.

But as a cultural theorist and a Christian, I'm concerned that these "value" issues seem to limit the conversation the Christian church has had with the culture. I'm less interested in the morality of Britney Spears than I am in the spiritual environment that spawned her. That is why I'm focusing on *California-ism*, which describes an entire belief system, the thought patterns behind all forms of conduct. Without our realizing it, these thought patterns influence everything that makes us human: our eating, our mating, our grieving, our historical chronicling, our laws, our worship, and more. California-ism *creates* Californication, and we must grapple with the cause before decrying the effect.

Moreover, California-ism creates something I will call a *Cal-type*, a kind of prototype manufactured with the essential features that humans might be expected to model within this belief system. In the following pages, I make a distinction between actual Californians, as I know them, and the Cal-type, which exists only in a mediated fantasy that we are often tempted to inhabit. The fact is, the church itself has not escaped the profound effects of California-ism, and without disencumbering herself of these beliefs, she has little or no chance of "redeeming culture." I have made both church and culture the subjects of this study, since both are dear to me. In some sections, I think my tone may seem angrier than I mean it to be, and I hope that will be forgiven. I'd be lying if I said I didn't feel a great sense of urgency, but that urgency stems more from hope than despair.

I wanted to write this book to help my students, and more particularly, my children, negotiate the spiritual minefield they have inherited, and like so many, to try to make some sense of what has befallen the country. I began this book in 2004, when Philip Cushman articulated the fears of some others. "Today," he wrote, "we are watching our democratic republic devolve into a crass, swaggering, self-deceiving empire."[2] Many will argue that point. But my concern is, whether or not we behave like an empire, do we believe like an empire? And if so, what is the effect on the personal, social, and spiritual lives of humans? I am studying a particular place, my home state, which I love very much, in order to extrapolate findings concerning the whole republic, because California, regardless of its heavy influence on the country, is also the repository of American values. The choice of the eagle as the national bird derived from the American desire to emulate the Greco-Roman Empire.[3] Empire values, namely personal freedom, pleasure, power, and perfection, have never been far from our door.

It seems impossible to divorce the Golden State's impact on the world from its effect on my personal life as a California baby. My own biography is in fact vaguely mythological and deeply metaphoric of my home state. As a preschooler, I was raised in Hollywood, across the street from ABC-TV, appearing on television not long after my family acquired its first TV as a prize my mom won from a TV show. From the time I entered kindergarten until I graduated from high school, we lived sixty miles farther out, in the semidesert of San Bernardino County. Somewhere in that sixty-mile transition between the Californian worlds of Beemers and bikers, surfers and skateboarders, somewhere around *Bill and Ted's* San Dimas, the landscape begins its slow but steady transformation into the apocalyptic vision of *The Mad Max Trilogy*. That setting was the backdrop to my formative years.

I moved to San Francisco to attend a protest-riot-torn state college and, as it turned out, to experience brief celebrity as a local performer then, inevitably, headed back to Los Angeles to experience brief celebrity in television comedy. Like Forrest Gump, I have met most of the major celebrities of my age, and have returned to where I started, utterly unchanged. I lived outside the state for the first time when I was in my thirties, when my husband and I attended graduate school in Kentucky. There I met a toddler at church who confided to me that he wanted to be a missionary to Mars or California. The comment struck me for several reasons.

First, he unknowingly confirmed my suspicions that I had grown up in some form of "outer space," even before the nationwide diffusion of the Planet Hollywood franchise. Second, at the time I was busily studying ways to rescue children from Hollywood's effects, while this four-year-old was calmly intending to rescue Hollywood itself. Third, even as I pictured the toxic gasses surrounding Mars, I sensed that California was in need of rescue, not so that it could align itself with the well-behaved Midwest but so that it could be revived from a deadly sort of stupor, one that anesthetizes us to actual human experience, relationship, environment, and, I fear, the true God. I began to wonder whether California's trance might not be a quasi-religious one and California itself the site of a weird kind of pagan religion, since it did not seem grounded in geography or history so much as ardent mythology.

I now teach a wide breadth of studies in popular culture at a faith-based liberal arts university. I also teach civic development. I am attempting to help our students reclaim cultural democracy in Southern California through the efforts of a tiny grassroots organization. It is a gargantuan task, made all the more arduous and precarious as I find myself, my students, and my community walking the line between reality and illusion like drunks trying to pass a sobriety test. The intention of this book, then, is to cast a critical if compassionate gaze upon the heavily commoditized artifacts and rituals of California-ism, in hopes that insight can be drawn from the interplay between personal history and corporate mythology.

Its greater intention is to encourage the reader not only to shake off the delusional and damaging effects of *California-as-a-contrived-religion*, but also to engage the promise of *California-the-created-region* in new and dynamic ways. Although California is a local phenomenon, California-ism is a universal one. Our inclination toward idolatry is the first one addressed by the Law of Moses, and California is the Ephesus of our age, feverishly dispensing new and improved idols by the crate load. While neighborhoods crumble, children suffer, war and disease ravage, and global warming devastates, we have gotten "sleepy, very sleepy," too sleepy even to make it to the voting polls, let alone Holy Communion.

Nevertheless, if our myths have an intoxicating effect, that effect might work in two different directions. An intoxicant can dull or invigorate. I believe one of the shortest ways back to connection with the real world, both seen and unseen, is through story/myths, art/artifacts, and meaningful rituals. Fraught with concerns as this book is, I mean to present redemptive possibilities inherent in our worst choices, as I recognize the eternal instincts and longings within these human activities. Ultimately, I'd like to find a way out of Oz and help others do the same. I hope we will conclude that, despite its perceived difficulty and dreariness, its lack of magic and Technicolor, there really is no place like home. Perhaps then we will turn our attention to our real environment, real community, real relationships, and real policies—personal, political, and spiritual.

2

State Spirit

Religion

When I was too young to voice any concerns, my family moved from Hollywood to Colton, California. Colton was located in what was once called the Inland Valley. As it developed economically, the region was renamed, significantly, the Inland Empire. Just an hour away in any direction glistened the tantalizing possibilities afforded by Sunset Boulevard, Disneyland, the Pacific Ocean, or the majestic San Bernardino Mountains. Colton was called "The Hub City," though it sort of felt like the middle of nowhere.

The Colton Cement Plant shadowed our town. It steadily pummeled a granite mountain to produce many tons of building materials and a constant cloud of dust that followed us home from school daily. The plant's dangerous-looking big brother, Kaiser Steel, spit its fumes from Fontana, overpowering the last scents of orange blossoms and making our hot walks home seem like those of the hobbits to Mordor in *Lord of the Rings*.

Over time, the semidesert culture of San Bernardino County produced more than its share of car shows, dance shows, car and dance shows, and strip malls. I remember returning from the grand opening of Colton's first strip mall with a free ice cream cone in hand. I told my mom the mall was okay, but I didn't think it would catch on. I felt somewhat more intimidated by the prototype McDonald's in nearby San Bernardino. In the early 1970s a cousin was to become the first female hired at McDonald's since the carhop layoff of 1948. I never much associated "gender equality" with the region, which is also an exceptional site for strip club billboards.

Eric Schlosser, in his book *Fast Food Nation*, calls San Bernardino "an odd melting-pot of agriculture and industry located on the periphery of the southern California boom, a place that felt out on the edge."[1] Schlosser notes that the postwar suburban growth in California encouraged mom and pop businesses to flourish in the sunshine of limitless opportunity. Mom and pop they have been, yet many of those same businesses morphed into multi-billion-dollar industries that suffocated imaginative competition in an unapologetic death grip. Schlosser quotes Ray Kroc, CEO of the McDonald's Corporation: "Look, it is ridiculous to call this an industry. This is not. This is rat eat rat, dog eat dog, I'll kill 'em and I'm going to kill 'em before they kill me. You're talking about the American way of survival of the fittest."[2] You want fries with that McDarwinism?

Anyone Hungry?

The same year that McDonald's was born, the Hells Angels (named after a US Army Airborne Division) also formed in San Bernardino, constituting what Schlosser considers the dark underbelly of the area's countless emerging franchises. He believes this part of California "supplied the nation with a new yin and yang, new models of conformity and rebellion."[3] My mother represented to me a well-scrubbed yet arbitrary and ultimately unattainable conformity. My father represented a solitary, violent, and hapless rebellion.

He too opened a business in San Bernardino, a barbershop. Dad was a pathological liar who specialized in overblown but sincere compliments. His business thrived. He was a stylish guy who'd pursued a career in broadcasting, and true to the entrepreneurial spirit of the Inland Empire, he developed a popular hair product that made a fortune for other people's children. Unfortunately, he gambled away both business and product rights in a poker game, long before poker became a national pastime. Dad had been dishonorably discharged from the military for impersonating an officer. He'd also undergone several name changes that may or may not have been criminal aliases in the east. My family was born under his short-lived show business name. Then as now, I equated our troubles with my father's discontent.

My school years were characterized by what seemed an impossible demand: excellence in the midst of utter chaos. After spending a late night looking for my dad in seedy bars or taking calls from his sentimental girlfriend, my siblings and I were expected to turn in grade-A homework while wearing tidy outfits. We joined our classmates in carefully folding our hands as we proceeded quietly under our desks during nuclear attack air raid drills, and this became an allegory for the rest of daily life. Like the *Titanic* orchestra musicians, we were to maintain our best behavior while water slowly engulfed drowning voyagers.

Actually, we were lucky compared to the children of the previous decade. During World War II, which introduced my parents to one another, California's children had been dog tagged. Poised on the Pacific Coast, California prepared for a Japanese attack similar to the one on Pearl Harbor. The result was "an army of air wardens, initially 33,000 in L.A., 20,000 in San Francisco, and 10,000 in San Diego."[4] Disaster preparedness took an interesting turn in California. "Historians have often believed that the outbreak of war made Californians hysterical"[5] but if so, it was a low-grade hysteria, quickly translated into a variety of jazzy yet tough-minded control mechanisms. These included yacht patrols, civil defense pageants on school playgrounds, posted warnings on glamorous beaches, and sham military battles in major sports arenas (sort of like those staged in the ancient Roman Coliseum). "Since loose lips could sink ships, urbanites were told to zip them, and bartenders and cosmetologists were encouraged to monitor compliance."[6]

During the cold war that followed, as California's defense industry continued to expand rapidly toward an uncertain and unstable future, California's wartime surveillance shifted into peacetime surveillance. Amid the general xenophobia engendered by a sudden surge of diverse populations, the John Birch Society was founded in Orange County to insure a well-behaved, ultra-conservative future. Meanwhile the State Assembly un-American investigating committee elicited secret testimonies. A group of screenwriters and directors known as the "Hollywood Ten" were called to testify before the McCarthy Hearings, and most were indicted and imprisoned for invoking their constitutional right to remain silent.[7] Hollywood's fear of blacklisting reverberated throughout Southern California and settled uneasily in the dust of the Inland Empire, where I too lived in dread of surveillance.

A Thirsty Land

One Sunday when I was around seven, my hair combed so tightly it gave me a headache, I was staring down at my organza dress with little purple flowers on a white background. I noticed that if I stared at it long enough, it looked like another little world and I was trying hard to reach that little world, far from the Inland Empire. The minister's wife was asking us to raise our hands if there was anyone there who had never sinned, and although I was uncertain what sin meant, I knew enough to keep perfectly still. However, another child raised his hand, and the minister's wife clarified, "You've never, ever lied to your mommy or been mean to your sister?" The child changed his mind and lowered his hand. "Uh-oh," I thought, and prepared myself for the worst. Sure enough, the minister's wife followed through with the information that we were all sinful, a concept

I still didn't really understand, but I knew it had something to do with why I was always in trouble.

The fact was, most of the time I'd had no idea why I was in trouble. I only knew that I would look up and suddenly someone—my mom, my babysitter, my teacher, or some other looming figure—would be headed my way with murder in her eyes. I'd make every attempt to correct my behavior, taking my best guess at what I was doing wrong. If I were standing up, I'd sit down. If I were sitting down, I'd stand up. If I had something in my hand, I'd get rid of it. If not, I'd grab something. And so on. "One more chance!" I'd cry, with a speech impediment so severe it rendered me unintelligible. But that chance was rarely granted. Yankings and spankings were swift and sure. Explanations, less so.

The minister's wife was telling us that Jesus had come to earth to be punished for us so we wouldn't have to be punished, and I heard that loud and clear. She told us we could close our eyes and ask Jesus to save us, and I did. As I recall, my heart was racing. When I opened my eyes, the Styrofoam cross with plastic flowers on the makeshift altar at the front of the room was shimmering, almost dancing. I didn't know the word for what I was experiencing, but it felt really exotic. I later learned it was grace.

Not long after that, my teacher at Lincoln Elementary School gave our class a serious assignment. We were to create an artistic work on the subject of conservation, and all the county's schools were competing. We were given a list of possible themes to explore through the medium of our choice. After careful deliberation, I selected from a list of suggested themes, "A Thirsty Land," making the daring decision to use chalk. I was given one large piece of white construction paper, and warned that there would be no replacements, so I was to map out my drawing in pencil. Drawing was not my strong suit. It had taken my teacher quite some time to show me why it was anatomically impossible for a woman to have arms growing out of her head. Still, I got busy with a tiny disc of a sun that I planned to color bright red, burning over a scorched brown desert landscape with large green cacti.

I held the chalk in my right hand and supported it with my left, with the perspiring brow of a brain surgeon. Jesus was helping me. Miraculously, the chalk was behaving itself and an actual picture was taking form. I thought the colors were especially effective. "A Thirsty Land," the girl next to me read aloud. She said it looked really good. In an outburst of artistic confidence, I decided to add a black shadow to one cactus. I did a poor job, not having planned properly, but I still kind of liked it. I was actually having fun in the desert. It was just the chalk and myself now, and I forgot about my hands, one of which was resting on the paper before I knew it.

When I lifted my fist, a black smudge occupied my perfect blue sky. I caught my breath and the room began to spin. I didn't know what the punishment would be, but I knew I was in trouble. Then something altogether unexpected happened. A kind of a voice told me, "That's okay." I honestly could not remember ever having heard that before, and I gratefully glanced up hoping to see my teacher, but she wasn't there. As I continued to blink tearfully at the picture, the red disc of sun blurred on the page, and I half involuntarily moved my finger toward it, then scandalously touched the chalk with my bare hand, gliding the edges of the red disc to cover the smudge. To my amazement, the soft blending of disc and smudge was making the picture prettier.

"You're messing it up," the girl next to me said loudly enough to make me jump. My teacher came over in response and looked at the picture with some surprise. She said it looked more like a real sunset now, and suggested I add a little orange and yellow. At the end of the week, my picture was chosen to represent my second grade class in the county competition and hung in a special exhibit at the San Bernardino Orange Show. It was the only honor I ever received in grammar school.

The Kingdom in the Empire

This personal account illustrates a central tension not only in my own spiritual formation but also in the spiritual formation of California. People seem drawn to California because it offers the very picture of gracious living—favorable and easygoing. Indeed, the possibilities for freedom, authenticity, renewal, creativity, and second chances abound here. But this gracious living comes at quite a cost; here we do not pass on the kind of grace dispensed by God. California's religious history and iconography, particularly the artifacts and rituals drawn from the Roman Empire via Catholicism, provide a case in point. Indeed, "local artists [represented] California missions as the New World counterparts of the Roman forum and the ruined temples at Agrigento and Paestum."[8] Jeweled and gilded saints initially modeled after Rome's gods and goddesses were enshrined at the missions in baked adobe and tile, reminding the faithful what perfected humans should look like before the celebrity industry took over.

The faithful paid then, as we often do now, a fairly high admission price to the throne of grace, though God was not cut in on the deal. In the case of the California Indians, this church enterprise ended up costing nearly everything they had. According to James Rawls and Walton Bean, "During the entire mission period, the native population from San Francisco Bay to San Diego fell from 72,000 to 18,000—a decline of over 75%."[9] The wide availability of land emptied of its original occupants resulted in a real estate promotion campaign that has continued ever since.

The culture of the Chumash tribe disappeared entirely, and we are left to guess at what their relationship was to the region we now call California. But based on the evidence, it appears that they were content to tend the place without altering it much. It also appears that their culture was steeped in religious ceremony. Later it would be concluded that the Chumash just weren't hard enough workers to deserve this place, though they had survived quite well and for quite some time.

The Spanish empire's acquisition of California was founded upon the mission system, a tortured confluence of church and state interests that established an uneasy truce in commerce. "For what purpose have we come?" wrote Father Pedro Font.

"To gain heaven by suffering trials in this world and . . . setting a good example of Christianity in the conversion of heathen whose souls are precious pearls sought by that celestial merchant, Jesus Christ."[10] Certainly a fellow merchant like Christ could be counted upon to understand the need for economic capital. Two summers ago, I heard a little girl who was eyeing a Coke machine in the Carmel Mission courtyard ask her mom, "Did they have money back then?" Well, yes, honey, they sure did. Of course, it depended on who "they" were.

Exploiting and ultimately destroying the native culture of California, the oppositional values of soul saving and economic expansion vied for prominence in early California. It might be concluded that the tension between these forces constitutes the ongoing dynamic of our state. One can never be sure to what extent California's essential makeup is somehow ordained by God; thus any man-made, self-interested choices driving the state might remain largely unquestioned.

"Manifest destiny" is still being exhibited in California. "The only quality that I feel pretty sure I have is my good intentions,"[11] admitted Juniper Serra, father of the mission system. "As to anything else, what means have I of knowing whether I am right or wrong?" Our ancestors gave themselves permission to proceed with good intentions on a seemingly spiritual but ultimately commercial enterprise, and drove recklessly, so to speak. The road connecting the missions was named El Camino Real, the Royal Highway—and it was unclear to me as a schoolchild who the royal referent was, the King of Heaven or the king of Spain. The devoted friars may have set out to spread the kingdom of God, but they laid the groundwork, as happens in so many crusades, for the empire of man.

As Walter Brueggemann observes, the principles of Christ's eternal kingdom are in direct conflict with the principles of man-made empires. The kingdom is based on grace, the empire on earnings. The kingdom is freeing, the empire binding. The kingdom is peaceful, the empire brutal. The kingdom is authentic, the empire deceitful. The kingdom is forgiving, the empire judgmental. The kingdom is renewing, the empire debilitating. The kingdom is imaginative, the empire predictable. The kingdom is filled with second chances and good news to the poor. The empire is filled with power, greed, and injustice. When it comes right down to it, the kingdom makes no earthly sense to us. As Christ tells us, it's "not of this world." But that doesn't mean we won't try to co-opt it anyway.

Spiritual Enterprises

While it was minding its own business, US forces seized sleepy Monterey Bay without firing a shot, and a state capitol of California was declared very near the site where Junípero Serra blessed the establishment of Spanish territory. The US government annexed California into statehood so rapidly that our state seal commemorates the act by featuring the goddess Athena springing from the head of Zeus. This is how political action is symbolized: it just seems to happen all by itself as a process of (super) natural selection in which no one is to blame or credit, really.

The state capitol, nicknamed the "capitol on wheels" because it changed locations so often during the turbulent years of the state's formation, landed for a brief period in Benecia, California. In the capitol building (now a State Historic Park) there still hangs a WPA art project based on a legend recounted by Bret Harte (*Mrs. Skaggs's Husbands and Other Sketches*). It pictures Father Jose Antonio Haro in harried conversation with the devil on what has since been called Mount Diablo. The devil is forecasting the future of California, notably its passage from Spanish to Anglo rule. Current Californians seem oddly unself-conscious that Anglo rule is depicted as a curse. Evidently, we just like the painting.

More often, the spiritual imagery in our state's infrastructure, governing agencies, commercial ventures, and advertising campaigns has been loaded with interplay between geographic/economic expansion and religious piety. The first gold mine, established in 1849 in the Poverty Vulture Claim, was called

"Priest Mine" after the priest ministering to Chilean miners there. An onslaught of forty-niners followed, including a large Mormon population that built a tabernacle similar in construction to that of Marshall's Gold Mill and made plans to head back for Salt Lake as soon as they struck gold.

Charles Christian Nahl's painting of *Sunday Morning in the Mines* separates "good miners" from "bad miners" as carefully as Michelangelo separated saints and sinners in his *Last Judgment*. Like many paintings of the era graphically asserting that "California could still be considered the Pacific prize—the providential reward bestowed on those who had conquered the great expanse of the continent,"[12] it is morally Darwinist. The most morally fit miners are the successful ones. It was important that Charles Crocker, the railroad baron who commissioned the painting, be made to feel morally superior in order to justify the staggering amount of wealth he'd accumulated by, among other things, mistreating the workers who built his railroad.

Every kind of business that can be imagined has made use of the word *mission*. Fullerton, California, never had a mission, but it did have an "Old Mission" citrus brand. Its citrus crate label, like others, employed an image of a genuine mission borrowed from its town of origin and plopped down in another location. A Perflex Radio ad actually likened its service to that of a mission bell that called the faithful to prayer.[13] It would be interesting to know how Forentino Naja would have responded, he who served as bell ringer at San Luis Obispo mission for seventy-four years, or Gregorio Silverio, who began to ring the bells at age eleven and continued for sixty-two years before passing the tradition to daughter and granddaughter. I wonder how easy it would have been to convince them that they had so much in common with the wireless radio company. It's as though the ad makers already knew that years later, cellular phone companies would be paying churches many thousands of dollars to allow them to plant receivers in the high crosses and bell towers on church grounds that would provide the best reception to company consumers.

In the window of an antique store in Ventura, California, I spied a two-hundred-year-old cross that may have belonged to the Ventura Mission lying between a banjo and a commercial cooler for Cervantes beer. Later that day, in San Luis Obispo, California, I discovered what had been the world's very first motel. It was fashioned as a tiny mission. A more famous nearby motel is the Madonna Inn, created by Alex Madonna on the interstate highway his company built in the 1950s—Highway 101, formerly The Royal Highway. Now thousands can speed along the route formerly trod by Father Serra's donkeys.

True to Serra's spirit, Madonna makes heavy use of religious artifacts. The color pink figures heavily in the decorating scheme of the Madonna Inn, the same pink medieval artists used to symbolize the original Madonna when representing Mary prior to the Incarnation of Christ. Pink turrets and towers house 109 rooms with specific motifs. The "Just Heaven" room can be occupied for a daily rate anywhere from $246 to $370. At the Madonna Inn, amid every form of ornate kitsch money can buy, a statue of Saint Therese shares a boutique window with high-priced polyester leopard skin pantsuits, and a portrait of Alex Madonna in a cowboy hat shares a Plexiglas cube with an artistic rendering of the Last Supper.

We may be many things in California, but, despite what the rest of the nation believes about us, we are certainly not irreligious. Not only are we the birthplace of alternative denominations such as the Four Square, Calvary Chapel, and Vineyard churches, California has more places of worship than the rest of the country combined, and many such places hold to an orthodoxy that would surprise some. Nonetheless, the crackpot mentality associated with our region of psychics, palm readers, and new-age-of-the-month clubs, maintains its share of outlets in Christendom.

One of our most famous spiritual entrepreneurs is Robert Schuller, the first to establish a drive-in church, the popularity of which set the foundation for what is now the Crystal Cathedral in Garden Grove. There one might enjoy theatrical spectacles that rival Broadway productions, as well as beautifully landscaped grounds that include statues of a friendly Jesus happily playing with children. The statues closely resemble the fare at nearby Disneyland. One can also visit a gift shop brimming with spiritual self-help slogans, many of which encourage us to pull ourselves up by our spiritual bootstraps, so to speak. Emblazoned upon a far wall are the words, "If you can dream it, you can do it!" (a phrase later to be co-opted by the Will Ferrell ice skating satire, *Blades of Glory*).

Not to be outdone in the tourist trade, Trinity Broadcasting Network has built "Trinity Christian City International" in Costa Mesa, California. Undaunted by California's energy crisis, or the general standards of taste set forth by Orange County, it glows with a lighting design that rivals the intensity of space ships, and boasts an array of statues and paintings that bring to mind the Vatican collection without the artistry. Want to take a little of that magic home with you? Visit the TBN website, featuring their Gold, Frankincense, and Myrrh Gift Shop containing over one hundred twenty thousand items. At the "Virtual Reality Theater" one can "take an intriguing walk through an actual recreation of the Via Dolorosa, the street in the old walled city of Jerusalem where Jesus carried His cross to Calvary." And speaking of travel, the center is "conveniently located near many world famous attractions and shopping centers," so "you can spend the whole day, or make your visit part of a complete vacation."[14]

When the Best Just Isn't Good Enough

The marriage of business and religion finds endless examples in California, from Cecil B. DeMille's biblical epics to megachurch media marketing, and it makes us unusually vulnerable to heresy, particularly since so few of our customs are grounded in deep tradition. Our central heresy of choice has much to do with our ongoing response to the gospel of grace. In general, Cal-types seem less interested in what God has given us than we are in what we're going to do to earn it, or to make it better, preferably both. At the castle home of media magnate William Randolf Hearst, which overlooks some of California's most beautiful land, our guide told us a comedian once quipped, "This is what God could do if he had your money."[15] Californians stumbled into a landscape of wonder that we likened to the garden of Eden, and there, for the most part, we have gone to work fixing what we've assumed God has left undone in our surroundings, our bodies, our fortunes, our souls, and most especially, in one another.

Before we reached statehood, we had designed our own version of paradise via the wrenching formation of gold mines, "California's first tragedy of development."[16] Swiss pioneer John Sutter had planned to build yet another empire, which he intended to call "New Switzerland" but he settled for the power attained through Sutter's Gold Mill. California is not nicknamed the Garden State, although some approached this vast garden with awe and faithfully tended it with humility and gratitude. Rather we are called the Golden State. Ironically, geologists estimate that 80 percent of California's gold is still in our mountains, despite the feverishness of our attack,[17] and gold continues to operate as our central metaphor.

When the children of Israel lost patience with God's provision in the wilderness, they constructed a golden calf of their own design, based on the values of the Egyptian Empire they had just escaped. Cal-types, in our turn, have constructed an entire golden state. We've cleaned out nearly every pocket of habitation, from the buffalo plains to the sardine bays, with warlike determination. Nature is messy. Cal-types like to streamline. Nature requires things of us. Cal-types like to make the demands. Nature makes us feel small. Cal-types like to feel big. The Pacific Ocean is fun to watch, but if we try to swim in it, we can get knocked around by waves and soiled by seaweed. On the other hand, we can make our own tidy swimming pools, temperature controlled. And maybe if we're not using the ocean anyway, we should drill for oil there.

Meanwhile, by controlling, rerouting, and even pilfering other water sources, we have, miraculously, turned acres of desert into gorgeous oases. Yet even the citrus groves and rose gardens that lured so many here were swept up in an environment that apparently rubbed us the wrong way. California has more constructed landscape than any state in the union.[18] Concrete and steel abound in our railways, roadways, freeways, highways, aqueducts, hydroelectric dams, skyscrapers, factories, entertainment centers, super malls, super domes, super arenas, bridges, tunnels, overpasses, and endless housing projects. An enormous suction machine in my neighborhood boasts the logo, "Moving Earth to Award-Winning Levels." The terrain moans and groans under our bulldozers in perpetual upheaval. Who needs earthquakes?

Now, I admit, this constant upheaval could be nothing but good old-fashioned progress. At its most gracious, faithful, and humble, well-planned development is something the state does uncommonly well, and environmental concerns are something for which Californians routinely lobby. But within empire mentality, Cal-type goals become precisely those of the Tower of Babel builders, to "make a name for ourselves," and in so doing, to climb our way to God, or godlikeness. The result of the Babel building project was the destruction of community and the loss of communication. By contrast, one of the signs that God's Spirit is in our midst at Pentecost is that people understand one another again.

Technologies "R" Us

The story of the Tower of Babel begins with a new technology. Folks had found a way to build with bricks, instead of adobe, just as we did in California. Empires rely on technologies, in fact, and here in California, we never met a technology we didn't like. We are well known for our devotion to and reliance upon the vast production of electronic images that swallow us whole. In one motel room at the Madonna Inn, the bed faces a wall-length mural of an early Californian scout furtively looking out over a high ridge at the rich valley below. Into the mural a television is bracketed, so it appears as though the painted scout is staring at the television. When our actual environment, even our manufactured environment, fails to live up to our desires, Cal-types create alternate universes via the photo, film, and television industries, and live in them much of the time.

Though less often associated with our state than those glamorous industries, two other life-changing technologies were developed in California. These were the aerospace and cyberspace (Microsoft) industries, spawned after we reached the end of America's available land, when space itself became our final frontier, as *Star Trek* put it. In this respect, maybe it's appropriate to call Californians spacey. For the real frontier, the real wide-open space, is within us. It is the endless ocean or desert of our unquenchable yearning. Our longing is not specific, yet it knows no bounds. Once again, Californians foreshadow all Americans. We are still hoping to strike it rich, still trying to get lucky. What we fail to realize is that we are already lucky. We are trying to win what we have already been given, hoping for a winning streak that will demonstrate our connection with an unseen force of goodwill. "Luck" is the counterfeit of grace, simple grace, available to all, which is precisely what we don't seem to like about it.

We do not have to compete for grace, mine for it, earn it, or pay for it. It does not come and go. We can only rest in grace, thus becoming agents of grace. The translation of *Sabbath* to the word "rest" does not describe the kind of rest that's meant. When one is being rescued from drowning, the lifeguard shouts, relax! That's one notion behind Sabbath. When we rest from our frantic labor, we are being asked to trust another that everything is going to be okay. We don't have to save ourselves; we are being saved. We do not have to fret and flail and snatch. We are being cared for.

Living in grace is *itself* the work to which we are called, and hard work it is too. We must fight for the gospel of grace today harder than the Galatian church had to fight in the days of St. Paul. Happily, and emblematic of our state's potential, it was a native Californian, the community-minded Josiah Royce, who coined the phrase "The will to believe."[19] At our best, this is who Californians really are—not gullible and silly, but people with the will to believe. As I tell my theater students, unless we are children, it is hard work to make (ourselves) believe. It is hard work to be nice to others when we have been warned against them. It is hard work to rely on the goodness of God when the evidence appears otherwise. It takes years of practice.

I'd give anything if Californians really could be as the nation has stereotyped them: laid back. To me, the California sea otter is the perfect symbol for the truly gracious living always inherent in our state's best possibilities. Once land-based animals, otters were slaughtered by the thousands for their fur in the general blood bath of economic expansion. Like other Californians, they went west, to the ocean, where they adapted, "went with the flow," and became stronger and more resilient. An otter once bumped against an aquarium window I was staring into and nearly knocked me down. It was the most powerful creature I'd ever encountered. Yet in its migration to the sea, the otter also became more charming and seemingly much more playful and relaxed. Resting on its back in the ocean, the otter drifts along tossed by currents so tumultuous that it disappears beneath the waves for minutes at a time before bobbing back to the surface, one tiny arm behind its neck, looking for all the world as though it should be resting a martini on its chest. This is the California waiting for us: this state, and this state of mind.

3

The Rest Is Mystery

History

"When legend becomes fact, print the legend."
The Man Who Shot Liberty Valance

My father was the most talented liar most folks in Colton knew. He once managed to convince the downtown druggist, a man who'd known my ultra straight and narrow mom since high school, that she was a drug addict, and that the suspicious prescriptions Dad was trying to fill were for her. My father's lies kept the family in plenty of hot water, but whether the loan company was coming to repossess our furniture during my birthday party, or the police were questioning my mom on our front porch, my first thought always was, "How does he do it?" It was as though he'd taken me by surprise all over again.

No matter how well acquainted folks were with the facts, my father was able to verify the fantastic. The first morning my mother spent with her in-laws, she discovered a note to his sister on which my dad had written a dozen untrue "facts" about his life. At the top of the list, he had scrawled "Things Helen

Believes About Me." What he did not add was that these were also things he believed when he said them. That's the power of pathological liars; they believe what they are saying, so others do as well. Maybe it was inevitable that my father would make his way to California.

The universal human problem of rendering accurate histories found particular challenges in America, particularly in the Wild West. The territory itself seems to require superlatives and extremes, especially in California, land of highest mountains, lowest valleys, oldest and tallest redwoods, most forbidding desert, wettest weather, driest weather, and most catastrophic rains, floods, fires, and earthquakes in the continental United States.[1] From the outset, it was an easy land to lie about, and so we have. But like the pathological liar, Cal-types believe what we're saying. And like the pathological liar, that makes us pretty convincing, and probably pretty unsafe.

"California entered history as a myth," writes Kevin Starr.[2] The fictional nature of the state meant that the stubborn facts of life were our enemy almost from the beginning, so we were prone to fabricate our experience. Once that happens, can we ever go back? Scores of writers have attempted to unpack the dynamics of California in a lucid, scholarly fashion, which demands distance and objectivity. Yet so many, like me, seem to tumble into a subjective narrative on the topic, further evidence that the peculiar power of the state is difficult to describe in the usual ways. While other states in the union typically are named after actual geographical locations (New York, New Mexico), historical figures (Washington, Rhode Island) or native tribes (The Dakotas, Massachusetts), California is named after the mythical queen, Calafia. In some respects, we seem to have been hovering above ground ever since, and inviting the rest of the country to do the same—an invitation that has been widely accepted and often enhanced by fellow Americans.

Queen Calafia is a character from *Las Sergas de Esplandián* (*The Deeds of Esplandián*), a Spanish romance written in 1510 by Garci Ordóñez de Montalvo. Calafia ruled the mythical island of California "very close to the side of the Terrestrial Paradise."

In the story, Californians "rode griffins into battle and fought with golden weapons" and Queen Calafia herself was "very large in person, the most beautiful of all of them, of blooming years and in her thoughts, desirous of achieving great things."[3] In 1533, Spanish explorers led by Hernán Cortés landed on what they thought was a Pacific island, and over time they called it California, "half believing they would find there as well the gold and precious stones described in Montalvo's romance."[4] Starr notes, "The Spanish in general had a tendency to conflate fact with fiction when it came to these prose romances."[5]

In that regard, they would find plenty of company in years to come. Today, Queen Calafia figures prominently in *Golden Dreams*, a high-end video presentation produced for Disney's amusement park California Adventure. Whoopi Goldberg brings Calafia to "life" as a holograph in a domed theater vaguely resembling a temple. There she introduces the truth about California, which we are about to see reenacted on screen. Calafia must wear several costumes in order to do California's history justice. Her larger purpose, it turns out, is to avoid detection as she invests figures from California's past with a Tinkerbellish fairy dust to give them the courage, insight, and magical resources to succeed, or in the case of minorities, to survive. The fairy dust, administered to the famous and obscure alike, is presumably the very spirit of California, some finely ground character traits of the mythic Calafia, she who was "desirous of achieving great things." Acting as our transcendent agent of grace, this fictional character from a medieval tale occupies no actual time, is not bound by chronological facts, and can jump from event to event without notice of causes or consequences. She serves only spectacle and feeling.

The video reminds me that during the 1950s, Walt Disney launched a genre of feature films he wished to call *True Life Fantasy*. According to *E-Ticket* magazine,[6] "Critics pointed out the philosophical contradiction between the terms 'true life' and 'fantasy,' so Disney dropped the phrase. He did, however, continue with the genre."[7] Unique in its ability to transform the actual, physical environment into an occupied fantasy, California Adventure was placed squarely within the true-life California and resulted in its infrastructural upheaval (dust, wreckage, rerouting of freeway traffic, etc.). The Adventure itself isn't exactly an adventure, since, as G. K. Chesterton reminds us, to have real adventure one needs a real person, rather than animatrons and the like.[8] The California Adventure is, instead, an attempt to replace the real California with a constructed image of California, as is our historic custom. Not surprisingly, there are mixed results.

A former street parade at California Adventure celebrating an implied sun god has given way to the Block Party Bash, where we can "rock with the Pixar Film Pals." And though there are quaint opportunities in the Adventure for tortilla tasting and wine sampling, the more popular attractions are high-sensation-seeking rides not to be found in the traditional, safety-conscious Disneyland next door. My favorite ride features an OMNIMAX dome screen into which park guests are air lifted, fans blowing in their faces, to simulate "Soarin' over California," from Golden Gate Bridge to Yosemite, to beaches, snow peaks, vineyards, golf courses, and back again to, best of all, the Magic Kingdom, where Tinkerbell awaits to welcome us. Soaring over California is very different from living through California. And this is the appeal. "The pleasure of imitation, as the ancients knew, is one of the most innate in the human spirit," writes Umberto Eco. Soaring over California, "we also enjoy the conviction that imitation has reached it apex and afterwards reality will always be inferior to it."[9]

Step Right Up

California Adventure Park is confined to the city of Anaheim. But at one time, the entire state of California was a kind of amusement park, fueled by the steady onslaught of heavily exaggerated advertising. This advertising was created by state boosters, and ironically, by the well-intentioned publication of Helen Hunt Jackson's 1884 novel, *Ramona*. Similar to Harriet

Beacher Stowe's goals in the writing of *Uncle Tom's Cabin*, "Jackson's noble aspiration was to create a work of fiction that would enlighten, inform and empower the American people to do something about the injustices toward Native American and Mexican Americans living in the turbulent Southwest,"[10] whose land had disappeared from under them.

However, readers were enraptured by the splendid scenic descriptions, the star-crossed romance, and the breathtaking adventures within a flamboyant, colorful, and largely imaginary Spanish past. They flocked to California from all over the world in search of the sites inhabited by the fictional Ramona. Thus, like Calafia before her, "the most important woman in California never lived."[11] Nevertheless, Ramona sites, brands, theatricals, artifacts, and roadside attractions—virtually anything that could be sold—were plentiful. If tourists were disappointed to learn that there was no real Ramona, the fictional Ramona still seemed to keep them coming.

This should have come as no surprise in a land whose history in the mid-1800s was less dominated by factual information (such as baptismal and legal records, or even land deeds) than by sensational narratives of violence involving notorious Mexican bandits such as Joaquin Murieta and Three-fingered Jack. The pamphlets, written by John Rollin Ridge and others, found a wide readership despite the fact that they contained a "fragility of evidence [that] anticipates the eclipse of fact by legend. The story of Murrieta began to displace the events that had given it meaning."[12] Focusing on the bad deeds of those native to the land drew attention away from the greater larceny whereby the territory was being steadily robbed from its inhabitants.

Californian narratives such as the Bret Harte stories of the gold rush "retail a past that can be warmly remembered" and trade "the pain of memory for the revisions of nostalgia."[13] Such memory loss allows us to overlook the ongoing societal injustices created by historical events. Stanley Hauerwas reminds us, "History often becomes an exercise in amnesia just to the extent that the wrongs of the past are forgotten or made part of a plot that suggests that everything has worked out for the best."[14] Walter Brueggemann's recommendation is not a return to traditionalism, but a return to memory, which he believes has been co-opted by a dominant culture that cannot afford to let people remember. In other words, our amnesia benefits the powerful, particularly the politically and economically powerful. This is an effect of what Brueggemann calls "the royal consciousness" of empire.[15] Similarly, Freud never saw amnesia as simple amnesia, but as a "remembering to forget."[16]

Though recent historical texts have attempted confessions about California's past—for example admitting to the slavery system that ran several missions and to the use of solitary confinement, whippings, leg chains, and stocks to control the native population—many missions themselves have fallen into disrepair or disappeared entirely. Schoolchildren in California are expected to remember the name of Father Serra, but little else. Instead, children (usually aided by their parents) often construct mini missions with a heavy concentration on aesthetics and production value. History as a meaningful subject has given way to the hard sciences under the No Child Left Behind Act, which in this case may mean that "no child is looking behind." Rollo May notes that Americans in general tend to regard history as insignificant and that many "secretly believe Henry Ford was right when he said, 'History is Bunk!' For him history began with the invention of the Ford flivver. Concerned only with the present and the future, our myth omits the actual richness of American History."[17] So here again, it's important to note that historical amnesia is not simply a statewide malady, but a national one. In any case, it is a delusional people that think we can have a present and a future without a past.

Will This Be on the Test?

Herbert Marcuse[18] believes that in certain pedagogies, memory is replaced by memorization. Standardization tells us what is important to remember, and as facts and figures increasingly have less and less to do with the material world around us which is always being transformed, the past seems to have little tie to actual experience. While our minds are busy storing endless streams of imposed information, we grab frantically for palm pilots, trying to retrieve the date of our best friend's birthday and worrying aloud, "Why can't I remember *anything*?" Day-Timers replace diaries as the record of our life's journey, and if I can see an event in my schedule, I can believe I was there. Under such circumstances, we are entirely reliant upon the very technologies that have co-opted our memories in the first place.

Of these technologies, the photographic image probably became the most powerful, though Californians had long been used to eyeing their own calamities from a distance. For example, early in our history devastating fires were so routine that onlookers became "arrested by the spectacle of catastrophe" and had "neither the time nor the inclination to analyze the social conditions that gave rise to so many of these conflagrations."[19] According to David Wyatt, the actual "conversion of catastrophe into spectacle," which tended to both obscure their consequences and raise morale,[20] depended ultimately on the emerging technologies.[21] Upon seeing Arnold Genthe's photograph of downtown San Francisco following the 1906 earthquake and fire, several people asked, " 'Oh, is that a still from a Cecil DeMille picture?' To which the answer [came], 'No, the director of this scene was the Lord Himself.' "[22] It would not be the last time the work of DeMille would be confused with that of the Almighty.

As a matter of fact, one of the more publicized archeological digs in our state is being conducted not to recover artifacts from our actual past, but rather artifacts from DeMille's 1923 production of *The Ten Commandments*, shot in the sand dunes of Guadalupe, California. Though one archeologist questioned the legitimacy of the project, Brian Fagan, an esteemed professor emeritus from the University of California at Santa Barbara responded, "Is not a modern ancient Egyptian palace an entirely legitimate target for archeological exploration?"[23]

Well, maybe; that is, if the term "modern ancient" is legitimate. Our landscape itself constructs memory and social identity, unless we destroy it, as we are prone to do throughout America and particularly in California. (In 1887, bankers grew alarmed because property changed hands so quickly no one bothered to record deeds.) When our landscapes and neighborhoods evaporate from beneath us to be replaced by bigger and better things, all reference points are lost. By and by, we forget what it was we were looking for, and the next thing we know, we are looking for history in a lost movie set: DeMille's movie about history.

Wyatt explains that in the progression from real event to filmed event, the world we see "is steadily internalized into a manageable and manipulable image. The sense of something staged, as if Genthe had taken a picture of people acting in a movie; the repetition of words like 'watching' and 'gazing' in Genthe's prose; the emphasis upon 'the attitude of the people' rather than on the content of what they see—all this marks the full emergence, on California soil, of the culture of spectacle." Later he adds, "Spectacle can be defined as the *use* of form that sets out to distance its audience from the represented event while mystifying that audience about the event's contexts and possible causes."[24] In a nutshell, this is the premise of a much later and very different movie from DeMille's: *Bill and Ted's Excellent Adventure*.

He's Famous, Dude—Let's Bag Him!

"History is about to be rewritten by two guys who can't spell." That was one tagline of the 1989 satire about two high school students from San Dimas, California, in danger of flunking history, with dire consequences to themselves and, as it turns out, the world at large. They are rescued when a visitor from the future provides them with the much-needed technology to time travel—a phone booth into which they cram assorted historical celebrities. Abraham Lincoln, Billy the Kid, Joan of Arc, Genghis Khan, Socrates, Beethoven, Sigmund Freud, and Napoleon are snatched out of historical context and thrown together into the electronic device that transports them to San

Dimas. (When Saint Joan is snatched away from her medieval environment, she is kneeling to pray before a crucifix. But she is *truly* amazed by the vision of the phone booth.)

In San Dimas, the historical figures will enjoy themselves at the mall and spend a little time in jail, while Bill and Ted prepare an entertaining presentation for their history final. In service to that entertainment, each historical celebrity will appear briefly on the high school auditorium stage to dazzle with a brief demonstration of skill, from swordplay to psychoanalysis, before communicating their enthusiasm for Bill and Ted, or San Dimas, or its pop cultural artifacts. In this environment, Billy the Kid gets along great with Socrates, Beethoven with Genghis Khan, and so on. Why shouldn't they? There's no mention of anyone's actual historical context, or philosophy or worldview or mission, no mention of cultural or social or political dynamics. As a result of magical technology, the figures are all just part of the same spectacular show.

By way of finale, Abe Lincoln steps forward to tumultuous applause, saying "Four score and seven hours ago, we your forefathers were brought forth upon a most excellent adventure, conceived by our new friends, Bill and Ted. These two *great* gentlemen are dedicated to a proposition that was true in my time, just as it's true today: Be excellent to each other. And, party on, dudes!" Then the historical celebrities reenter the phone booth and disappear, creating one more special effect. As a history project, they are a big hit and Bill and Ted can stay in school, so that their rock band can develop the sound that will be used to govern the future world.

The film lampoons several cultural assumptions, among them the assumption that historical figures would envy and admire us despite any of our shallow ineptitude, as embodied by the vacuous Bill and Ted; that thoughtful study and artistic skill can be replaced by the right technologies, so long as those technologies land in the hands of really nice dudes; and most importantly, that history can be controlled and manipulated to serve our needs. As Ted puts it, "Our historical figures are all locked up!"

The actual history of San Dimas is more interesting to some of us. San Dimas was named after the thief who hung on the cross next to Christ, professing faith in Christ there and receiving absolution and eventual sainthood. The priests of San Dimas invoked this saint's name because renegade horse thieves populated the area, and the priests wished to convey to them that Christ forgives thieves. This forgiveness is a far cry from the magical rescue of nice guys like Bill and Ted, upon whom history shines approval. If Cal-types play our cards right, most of us still believe we can substitute forgiveness with forgetfulness.

Currently, many Californians, and, here again, many Americans, are not even sure about what it is we're supposed to forget. Wyatt believes the widespread use of photography meant that "between the claims of voice and the power of spectacle, those who lived in Southern California would henceforth make their unsolitary way."[25] That unsolitary way is now littered with fact-altering devices over which the younger generation must stumble incessantly. I was first made aware of the students' reliance upon image to verify, or create, history some years ago when I began to notice a pattern in their speech. They would say things like, "Well, Dr. Ganas, that's *always* been true. Clear back in the 1950s, thus and such . . ."

"The 1950s?" I'd tease. "That's the dawn of man?"

As we conversed, I realized "history" in the minds of many students began with the television era, and that which was verifiable was really only that which was televised. Thus the Kennedy assassination was more trustworthy as an historical event than the Lincoln assassination, the facts of which were passed down through personal accounts, much like the facts of scripture. "The claims of voice" are ever more distant and muffled and finally ignored, regardless of whose voice. Specific human events (such as those recorded in Psalms), events that have been truly and deeply experienced and that may prove truly and deeply meaningful to a listening community, give way to glib and arbitrary generalities or trends that can be mass produced and mass marketed as history. As has been observed, "Mass media placed their version of the senses' order upon existence. As the word, the image is reproduced again and again, it becomes fact, known simultaneously by strangers. It is the lifeblood of a mobile world system employing standardized meanings and requiring standardized understandings. Fact is seen over and over again, repeated by itself and others. When stored, it becomes history."[26]

In the calculus of the television industry, the history of popular commodity culture is the most important history of all, and if the programming onslaught is great enough, the history of pop culture will become the only history we know. In fact, as scholar Svetlana Boym observes, "Unless you are a hopelessly nostalgic foreigner, you cannot even long for anything outside of popular culture."[27] And even pop nostalgia must be controlled.

Remembering and Dismembering

The opposite of remembering is dismembering, and one cannot do both rightly at the same time. Yet this contradictory process is precisely what must happen to a history that is being segmented, packaged, and sold. Consider the decade nostalgia promoted by VH1, and the arbitrary slicing of time by decades to create such compilation-friendly genres as "'70s music" or "'80s music" that have nothing to do with style (country, jazz, etc.), only time period. We might presume that these time periods involve actual, individual lives and that the music of these decades is purchased to facilitate nostalgia for particular historical events, such as a high school prom.[28] What then, do we make of Kelly Rowland's commentary in *I Love the 70s*, she who was born in 1981? The implication is that a time period can be reminisced (or reexperienced) as though it has been lived firsthand because it has been *seen* on VH1. History can be appropriated to one's own past by purchasing the right pop cultural artifacts.[29] History itself can bask in celebrity as decades become the stars of their own shows.

Through the persistent fragmentation of visual attention, and a recommercialization of the already commercial, a "new historicism" has been minted, one that assumes history need not be lived, learned, or understood, but simply bought. Like Bill and Ted, Cal-types certainly don't need any relatives or teachers or historical societies or legal documents to get in the way of setting the record straight. Who needs historical records when we have recordings? After all, Cal-types don't even need our own life stories. We have Danny Bonaduce's. No matter how trivial or mediocre, it doesn't matter what information is worth remembering, but rather that it simply will be remembered. *Remembering* becomes the major goal, because what is really being robbed from us and sold back is the capacity for public memory itself. And that's what we're probably nostalgic for: a time when we were capable of memory, and did not need to invest, for example, in the scrapbooking aids of Creative Memories, Inc.

It may be easy to shrug off the sheer goofiness of VH1 and the like, but often viewers are less skeptical of other pop fabrications such as the televised docudrama, which intentionally fictionalizes history without most viewers' awareness. By creating such devices as the "composite character" (a character that never really existed in historical fact, but is, rather, a composite of several actual people), the story presents itself as factual. The same principle applies to plot line. Because it is "based on a true story," nearly any truth will do. The Coen Brothers drew attention to the ethical problems of assigning this phrase to a movie when they attached it to *Fargo* and later declared openly that this was untrue, demonstrating how easily the public could be misled without repercussions for the filmmakers. In the age of the docudrama, which tends to be produced too speedily and researched too little, due process can be threatened or political decisions sanctioned before all the facts of an historical event are in. By the time the real story is told, few are listening. We think we already know what happened.

Tall Tales

With insight, humility, and courage, writer/director John Sayles (along with Eric Foner) has drawn our attention to the inherent

problems of translating history into film, regardless of how ethical the filmmaker attempts to be.[30] The medium itself presents
time constraints, financial issues, and artistic concerns that will
necessarily impede upon historical fact. But there is a significant difference between the humble attempt to film a historical
drama that presents itself openly as *a* story (hopefully intended
to engender discussion), rather than as *the* story (usually meant
to exclude discussion). When is history being lassoed for us,
and sometimes from us, and then sold back to us in a highly
controlled form that domesticates the imagination and discour-
ages inquiry? Does the story spring from the community under
discussion, or is it imposed upon that community?

Naturally, there is a slippery relationship between the everyday
"facts" of life within a community's culture and the accounts
of those facts within popular culture. Mass media's ability to
transform the factual material of everyday life into marketable
fiction may be a recent phenomenon, but there is a basic—and
ancient—human impulse being exploited here. Humans make
stories of their lives. The word *fact* comes from the Latin "fac-
ere" (to make or do), while the word *fiction* comes from the Latin
"fingere" (to make or shape). In some Latin-based languages,
the same word is used to mean "to do" or "to make." History
can refer to "things done" or to the things "made" of things
done, but "the very word 'story' lurks in the word 'history' and
is derived from it. What begins as investigation must end as story.
Fact, in order for it to survive, must become fiction. Seen in this
way, fiction is not the opposite of fact, but its complement. It
gives a more lasting shape to the vanishing deeds of men."[31]

As the philosopher Alasdair MacIntyre puts it, "Man is in
his actions and practice, as well as in his fictions, essentially a
storytelling animal."[32] It is the purpose behind the storytelling
that must be examined. Stories may be told by the dominant
culture in order to hide the truth and manipulate the facts.
But stories also may be told in order to discover the truth and
interpret the facts. Walter Fisher argues that narrative involves
the whole mind, resolving false divisions between emotion and
reason, and factoring "intuition" into "rational thought."[33]

According to Fisher, we should expect to find larger purposes and good reasons behind our stories, and at least some vestige of public moral argument, which is concerned with life and death issues, decency of human treatment, and desired patterns of living.[34]

Fact, Fiction, Faction

The blurring of fact and fiction is the subject of several important independent films of the 1980s, including *The Thin Blue Line* and *The Ballad of Gregorio Cortez*. Such films not only challenge our perceptions of "real" documented and historical events, but also question our very ability to perceive such events accurately in American life. These films served as important reminders of our human fallibility and our tendency to rework historical fact to our own advantage. But not long after, mainstream fictional film treatments of prominent biographies such as *JFK* and *Malcolm X* drew intense scrutiny and criticism for challenging our popular perceptions of more prominent historical figures.[35]

During the angry controversy over the film *JFK*, the *Los Angeles Times* quoted communication scholar James Carey as saying, "The categories of fantasy and reality have never been isolated, but now the distinction has collapsed." Sandra Ball-Rokeach echoed a nearly identical statement and also worried aloud that impressionable viewers might become confused about "the truth."[36] For his part, *JFK* director Oliver Stone claimed that the Warren Commission Report should be considered just "one more story" about the Kennedy assassination, and Nora Ephron joined Norman Mailer in arguing that "there is no such thing as truth." There were "only stories."[37]

At that time, the dialogue between filmmakers and communication scholars appeared to reflect a sincere if somewhat overdue concern about the power of visual mass media, and in particular the powerful combination of narrative and factual events. The problems presented by mass culture seemed honestly worrisome to us, a matter for heartfelt public discourse. It didn't last. Academics still worry occasionally, but it's harder to hold an audience. Eventually, we seem to have shrugged our shoulders, as we do over so much in American life, and gotten back to work, amnesia victims with a dim awareness of our former identities and lives. Not long ago, an ad for the "Hollywood Reporter" section of the *Los Angeles Times* crowed, "We live the movies!" On the other hand, on the same kiosk, the same newspaper promised us "The Real News."

When our historical assumptions are drawn from movies, our political assumptions can be as well.[38] In *The History of Forgetting*, Norman Klein reminds us that public policy and political action often have been thwarted in California by our inability to face fact or even recognize it.[39] Sometimes I think this accounts for our taste in governors. Ronald Reagan may have been dubbed "the great communicator" because he appealed to our cinematic imagination; that is, he sounded like the movies.[40] Now the dismantling of domestic programs that accompanied his administration is remembered by many in a gauzy, dreamy light, like the western sunset into which he seemed to ride. With the disappearance of public mental health facilities, among other much-needed programs, the mentally ill homeless who now roam California's streets share something in common with most of their fellow citizens. Not many can say exactly how it happened.

A more recent gubernatorial movie star, Arnold Schwarzenegger, is making an honest effort to address the state's many social and environmental issues, and he may be justly remembered as a good governor. Early in his administration, however, he owned an impressive collection of Humvees and once oversaw a tax rebate for SUV owners as gasoline prices soared, before declaring the less intrepid "economic girlie men."[41]

To my knowledge, there is only one popular film representation of the usurpation of Southern California's public transportation system (once one of the nation's finest) by auto manufacturers and freeway lobbyists. The film is *Who Killed Roger Rabbit?* It is a novel combination of cartoon and live action, fantasy and historical event (the dissolution of the red trolley line), presented in such a way that the viewer cannot reasonably assume that any such villainy really did occur. Instead, the trolleys are now viewed, not as a vital component of civic welfare, but as an attraction in Disneyland's "Toon Town."

Imagine attempting this in the treatment of other serious historical events, such as the struggle of labor unions, or maybe the depiction of the Civil War. Such attractions, or distractions, "overload our senses in an uncritical way."[42] There's no time to think, because here comes the next sensation! History in this context is meant only to amuse. I myself have been involved in glossy representations of social issues during my work in Hollywood, and I am all too well acquainted with the system by which complex, important concerns are rerouted into whimsical diversions. When the public is longing for stories of any kind, and actual stories are difficult to tell well, it is just plain easier to manufacture propaganda, especially in an environment that equates time with money rather than history. Nevertheless, there are redemptive approaches to storytelling for us to consider, and, I am proud to say, many are produced in California.

Theater over Theatrics

Since humans are natural storytellers, a better way to go is to try some stories that aim to reveal the truth behind the facts, rather than mask it. Stories tell us not only what events occur, but how they felt and what they meant. Such things are naturally subjective and when stories are forthcoming about their subjectivity, rather than masquerading as purely objective accounts, we are given the opportunity to evaluate various versions and form meaningful conclusions. We should also be wary of stories that concentrate *only* upon how events felt or what they meant. Before we know it, we will forget that the *Titanic* actually sank and why it actually sank, because we are too busy concentrat-

ing on the soundtrack-infused love affair between the fictional
Jack and Rose.

Real histories are messy, time-consuming, and laborious.
They are dynamic and often surprising; usually, they require us
to live with tremendous ambiguity before clamping down on
conclusions. When stories are too obvious, too quick, or too
simple, something's amiss. We suppose that in courts of law,
the more witnesses or perspectives are available, the closer we
are likely to come to actual historical evidence. This mirrors
the biblical assumption that the more important the story, the
more accounts are included in the canon; hence, we have four
versions of the gospel. I believe when people are given the opportunity to recount their own experiences, if anyone is listening, they are generally likely to reveal not all truth, of course,
but *some* truth. For this reason, I am a big fan of efforts such
as the Shoah Foundation, described as "History Told by Those
Who Lived It."

In the making of *Schindler's List*, Steven Spielberg and company found there were many Holocaust survivors who wanted
their stories told. Most had survived the camps solely in hopes
that they would live to tell their stories one day. Yet, when survivors arrived in the states and other harbors of safety, they
were encouraged to move on and put stories of the past behind
them. The Shoah Foundation provided the opportunity, through
donors and volunteers, for their stories to be recorded in full
and the data stored. As with similar efforts across America, such
histories could be used to provide missing pieces to historical
puzzles that would be useful in trying criminals or reuniting
families.

The "Living Newspaper" of the 1930s depression era, a
critical time for truth telling in America, provides a less direct,
more theatrical means of engaging personal and public histories
in multifaceted and compelling ways. The art form was developed by the short-lived but significant Federal Theater Project,
a government-sponsored venture helmed by Hallie Flanagan
Davis from 1935 to 1939. Integrating factual data and dramatic
vignettes, dialogue is taken from newspaper stories, as well

as speeches and similar documents. The intention is to bring problematic events to life, where their causes and possible cures can be explored.[43]

The Living Newspaper borrows several techniques from the Epic Theater of German dramatist Bertolt Brecht. Brecht loathed the notion of an uncritical audience that came to the theater for a cathartic emotional experience and left thinking they had performed their social duty by weeping for the (like-able) victims rather than taking some action to promote justice, or freedom, or any of the other human rights threatened by the Third Reich. Thus, like the Living Newspaper, he found ways to stylize his stories overtly, to ground history in art, and employ the Expressionist's tools of symbol, lighting, color, angle, distance, and minor notes to communicate emotional consequence without permitting emotional release. It may be worth mentioning that Hitler considered Expressionism a degenerate art form and banned its use.

Historical inquiry looks for possibility rather than inevitability and approaches subjects artistically rather than scientifically.[44] Many current dramatists combine elements of Living Newspaper and historical documentation, or documentary, when handling vital historical events. The effects are usually profound. Anna Deavere Smith's *Twilight* deals with the so-called Rodney King Riots in Los Angeles, 1992, and the many voices she includes provide insights and reveal psychological truths that might actually make a historical, political, or cultural difference. Luis Valdez's *Zoot Suit* explores another Los Angeles riot, located in the 1940s Mexican American community. The comedy troupe Culture Clash (Richard Montoya, Ric Salinas, and Herbert Siguenza) reveals in *Chavez Ravine* the unknown facts behind Dodger Stadium and the uprooting of the Mexican American community for the stadium's construction. Such drama encourages reflection and will not substitute image for imagination.

Along the way, we may imagine alternate scenarios, those that might yet be attempted. If these shows seem agenda-laden or propagandistic, we should remember that Jacques Ellul defined propaganda in terms of telling mass audiences what they want to hear.[45] This kind of drama operates in the opposite direction. It does not promise to be completely reaffirming to audience expectations, and that's the very point. If we listen to these stories, for they *must be heard as well as watched*, we may decide we have been self-satisfied too long. This is drama that does not intend to leave us as it finds us, and in that respect, it resembles high art.

There are countless such shows cropping up all over a city that now boasts of 240 theater companies, which is especially surprising since Los Angeles isn't considered a theater town. One of the most interesting endeavors is Cornerstone Theater Company. Founded by a small group of Harvard students that sought to make theater an integral and relevant aspect of ordinary American life, the company collaborates with community members to discover what themes emerge from their everyday experiences and personal histories. Then, with actors drawn from the community, they've created shows that are epic interactions between classic plays and specific American communities: Moliere's disintegrating and combative families in the Kansas farmland, Shakespeare's civil strife in the streets of Mississippi, and Aeschylus's ancient rituals on modern Native American reservations. Cornerstone has also featured a group of former steelworkers from Bethlehem, Pennsylvania, performing in a modern adaptation of *Prometheus Bound*, hard hats and all, and the *Optimistic Civil Servant*, featuring LAPD, public library, postal service, and public transportation employees.

By writing local concerns into the scripts, involving the community in key roles, and building local references into costumes and sets, Cornerstone Theater tries to tell truthful stories about real things, often playing to capacity audiences who are gaining rich insights into everyday experience, understanding other people, challenging prevailing injustices, and recognizing that artists are a part of the neighborhood. Cornerstone Theater's unique approach has attracted considerable support. As a result, it has been able to establish a working capital reserve; productions are mounted in larger venues; and the number of performances has increased. Perhaps most important, it now has the resources to sustain the local momentum it creates. Writing, directing, and production workshops are being offered to community cast members and other interested citizens. "By giving people the tools they need to mount their own productions, we are helping to support a flourishing tradition of performance in every community we touch," notes Cornerstone's managing director, Leslie Tamaribuchi.

Since moving to Los Angeles in 1991, Cornerstone has created and performed productions in concert with neighborhoods from Watts to Chinatown to Angelus Plaza, a low-income housing project for seniors. One production, *Los Illegals*, featured several undocumented workers telling their own, often-wrenching stories in Spanish. "We began with only an idea of the diversity of our nation, and we have been welcomed into a rich and specific tapestry of human lives, cultural realities, and community connections that continues to humble us with its breadth. We began with only an idea of the vitality of theater, and have discovered again and again that exhilarating, far-reaching works of art can be created when people come together."[46] Again, this is the California, and the America, waiting for us.

Living History

Though historical amnesia, while especially vivid in California, is an ongoing *national* temptation, it need not be a national failing. It is natural that we organize both the minor and major historical events of our lives into stories, but not necessarily into spectacle or product. Native Americans knew that they could retain no cultural power if their stories were corrupted, and most were careful to provide very little narrative to those who wished to conquer them. Understanding how and why we create our stories and who benefits from the process are more important than ever in the American empire promoted by California-ism. The move from powerlessness to agency lies in the ability to narrate our own stories, but first we must acknowledge them for what they actually are. They are comprised of a series of days, one day after another: from the time of Abraham to the time of Christ, to the time of you and me—one day following the next. The days need to be noticed, "numbered" as scripture puts it. "Teach these things to your children, and your children's children," we are told. *These* things, the stories that matter to the struggling immediate community, not to the surrounding empires. *These* things should be recorded in our minds and hearts: things that promote faith, a future, and a hope.

I am moved by the Jewish prisoner in *Schindler's List*, a literature and history professor, who believes the Nazis will value his profession enough to keep him alive. He is the first to go. I am also moved by the fact that during the Bolshevik Revolution, the best storytellers throughout the Russian landscape were tricked into a storytelling contest located in a massive barn that was locked and torched. The Bolsheviks rightly understood that as the stories go, so goes the culture. In many cautionary tales of the future, such as *Brave New World*, *1984*, and *The Time Machine*, history has been rewritten or forgotten, and must be retrieved in order to locate the culture's problems and their solutions. We need to retrace our steps, or act them out if we must. We need to "come to," as any amnesiac does, and realize we didn't land here magically.[47] Where we are today is the result of human choice, or human bondage, and so is where we will be tomorrow.

I learned that in history.

4

Extreme Reality

Television

Outside a séance parlor, it would be hard to find as spiritual a medium as television. Television architect Philo Farnsworth called it a divine invention, adding that God would severely punish those who misused it. In California television is often discussed in quasi-religious terms,[1] which reveals as much about us as it does about television. In church we were warned not to sacrifice to television time and attention that belonged only to God, little knowing this was but the tip of the iceberg. Television is not merely another means for conveying information, ideas, and entertainment. The ability to transport humans (or at least their actions and signs) through the airwaves, to cut across time, space, and solid matter, is, after all, a metaphysical activity.

Most folks seem to know there is no such thing as reality television. The moment something is photographed and transmitted, it ceases to be real in any conventional sense. So why are we so convinced that "the camera cannot lie"? Why does the televised world seem so much more *real* to us than our natural surroundings? This is not simply the result of overexposure, though on average we spend more time watching television than we do engaging our environment or one another.[2] There is something more. Television enables us to transcend our environment, catching glimpses of a "world beyond," and just as Eastern mystics obtain Nirvana in the final acknowledgement that "all is illusion," our technologies invite us to travel ever nearer to the same conclusion: TV isn't the illusion, life is.

As a little kid, I literally grew up on television, making early appearances on children's programs before I became a regular viewer. During one such "live broadcast" the host ran under time so he ad-libbed the final minutes to commercial break by asking us kids what we wanted for Christmas. I panicked, for I had never actually spoken on television and in fact had such a severe speech impediment that I was unintelligible to those outside my family. When he reached me I shyly told the host I wanted a bride doll, but he understood me to say a rag doll. That is what he bemusedly communicated to the home audience and, I imagined, to Santa Claus, who as a mystical creature had much more in common with television than with me, a tiny human without basic communication skills. I was powerless and my heart sank. I was sure Santa would bring me a rag doll, for my fate, my reality, lay in the supernatural airwaves.

This interplay between the ethereal broadcasting world and everyday life was a familiar one to me because our tiny home was crammed with prizes my mother had won from *Queen for a Day*, a major media event of its time. *Queen* was a show in which "ordinary" women competed by speedily sharing and comparing personal life stories, followed by a modest public request based on need or desire. Unlike other game shows, *Queen* seemed to require no particular skill or knowledge, only a woman's willingness to present her plight openly and naively, in a winsome way. The rest relied upon the capricious favor of powerful producers who would select contestants and audiences that would vote by the applause-o-meter.

Though the show is generally maligned and ridiculed, its effect still ripples through American culture with unusual force.[3] Like so much early programming, *Queen* was a prototype for so-called reality shows, because television was still drawing heavily from reality rather than creating it. *Queen* was also the first makeover show, the first use of the airwaves to "transform" the lives of humans, most of them Californians. In an industry that finds longevity surprising, *Queen* lived nearly twenty years—from World War II to the Vietnam era—and crowned over five thousand queens. Within its first three months, it was America's top-rated radio program, and by 1956, following its debut on television and boasting a daily viewership of thirteen million people, *Queen* was "daytime TV's all-time biggest hit."[4] With an emotional fanaticism often associated with the younger audiences of teen idols, members of the *Queen* studio audience would faint regularly and be carried by ushers to the rear of the auditorium.

Into this pungent arena wandered my unsuspecting mother. My dad, having joined the starry-eyed stream of immigrants to Hollywood in search of a broadcasting career, was curiously enough the only one of us never to make it to the airwaves. He changed his Irish-sounding name, making our new surname exactly one generation long, and proceeded to try his show biz luck. When he had none, he left California, abandoning my mom with two preschoolers and a baby on the way. (He wasn't gone for good, however.) Mom was a hardworking nurse who came home at night to scrub diapers in the bathtub. She reasonably yearned for a washer—nothing fancy.

The day of my mother's coronation was her first day off in quite a while. My aunt, hoping to raise Mom's spirits, hired a babysitter, and the two headed for the bus downtown. But, passing the crowds at the studio in our neighborhood, my aunt cried "Hey! Let's go see a show." And when my mom worried about the sitter, she laughed, "Who's going to know?" Who indeed. My mom ended up broadcasting revelations she hadn't told her own mother. (As it turned out, my grandmother was listening to the show but did not recognize Mom's voice, much less her problems.)

As she was spirited away from the studio "to begin her reign," Mom tried to tell the emcee that her sister was in the audience waiting for her. But no such trivial concerns would do for her highness. She was compelled to ride around the block, our very neighborhood, on the bench seat of a new Cadillac with a Ha-

waiian recording artist named Hilo Hattie. My mom, in full
regalia, waived gamely at our confused neighbors before being
dropped off back at the studio, where she turned in her finery
and signed necessary documents. When all was said and done,
she walked home.

We received a photo of her in housedress and ermine robe,
hairnet and tiara, seated on a flashy throne flanked by two
blonde models in fishnet stockings. "The one in the middle is
my mom," I would explain to neighborhood playmates. Then we
would grab a snack from the refrigerator provided by *Queen*, and
turn on the television or phonograph provided by *Queen* before
heading outside to play on the gym provided by *Queen*. My life
was brought to me by television, and that's not so uncommon
in and around Los Angeles, which is largely a company town.

Much of the news in the *Los Angeles Times* concerns the
entertainment industry, which employs much of Los Angeles
County's population. Though not everyone has a TV studio in
their neighborhood, the chances of interacting with television,
as a studio audience at least, are pretty great and our streets and
public spaces are routinely used as location sets. Later, we see our
towns on television, creating further evidence that we ourselves
hover above ground in the airwaves. Though we like to scoff at
the assumption across America that average Californians hobnob
with celebrities, the fact is that we do encounter more than our
share. We drive the same roads, shop at the same supermarkets,
and pay the same utility companies. It's just enough to make us
the perfect candidates for the reconfiguration of reality from immediate environment to electronic image. The implication is that
we ourselves must become larger than life in the transition.

The Queen for a Day Club

As an adult, I located over twenty other former queens, including
the very first. The queens had formed a club and adopted as their
slogan "Queenly *Forever*." They welcomed me warmly, called me
Princess Monica, and hoped my mom could make it soon. Meet-

ings were held at the regal-sounding Sir George's Smorgasbord in a suburban strip mall, where they had a crowning ceremony by lottery, and that day's queen opened a wrapped gift "just for fun." Then we had a smaller gift exchange—nothing over two dollars, so everyone had a little something to take home. Soon we got down to business and turned in whatever we had collected in our fundraising efforts for Los Angeles Children's Hospital, the real reason for our gatherings—to give something back.

I saw strength and charm in these women, not at all the whining, sniffing, unstable stereotypes our culture attached to *Queen* winners. Various members had great anecdotes, scrapbooks, and memorabilia from "the best day of their lives," including a *Queen for a Day* Storybook Doll, engraved silver scepter or velvet pillow, and dozens of glossies. But what really interested me were the common threads running through their respective accounts of the experience, which resembled a kind of fairy tale used to make sense of life.[5] In later years, *Queen for a Day* was subtitled "The Cinderella Show."

Queen offered the unimaginable: celebrity in the home. A woman could become famous while remaining a housewife, but the experience, intended to end at midnight, was a singular one. During the twenty-year run of *Queen*, hundreds of thousands of average women, like Cinderella's stepsisters, failed to fit the cultural mold that might make their dreams come true.[6] There could be only one queen and the losing contestants, who sometimes "burst into tears," were scrupulously left off camera.[7] The show embodied the ongoing competition and social Darwinism of most reality shows and of Hollywood itself. Not all former queens described their victory as "winning." Several said they were "chosen," as though through a process of natural selection, or divine election, or some uncanny combination thereof. Indeed, it may have become nearly impossible to distinguish between the two.

The power of *Queen* rested in its ability to convey overwhelming private and public favor in response to a woman's communicated reflection of self. Having a story worth hearing could enable a woman to attain celebrity, when in many cases survival was the original goal. The very act of appearing on television implied that one's real story, thus one's real life, mattered. Queens used stories to solve their immediate, circumstantial problems, and in doing so successfully, they empowered themselves in far more lasting ways. The fact that network producers also used queens' stories for personal gain seemed natural to them. The women I met did not feel remotely mawkish, humiliated, or ill used. They felt accepted, affirmed, and blessed. Apparently, they felt blessed not because they received something they did not deserve, but in a sense, because they received something they did deserve. The show promoted the notion of "earned grace" that seems to be increasingly at home in various California churches.

The queens generally had demonstrated conventional female virtues of patience, sacrifice, and dependency during their *Queen* appearance.[8] Yet the tale they related about that experience was frequently described in heroic terms involving a journey and conquest rather than in the passive terms commonly associated with feminine tales. The conventional tale would add that they lived happily ever after, presumably to be returned to life's margins and never heard from again.[9] However, these women refused to go away. Several went on to do other television shows as a result of their successful *Queen* appearances, and some, after forming the *Queen for a Day* Club, enjoyed intermittent public attention, from parades to media coverage, ever after. They resisted the fleeting nature of their "one shot at glory" and the fact that they formed a club, kept a monthly journal with messages from all members, and were ever vigilant for more members—other queens—suggested a rejection of the singular, isolated status imposed upon them as Queen for (only) a Day. Instead, they formed an interconnected community that was liberating and empowering.[10] Their real lives were far less Darwinist than life on the airwaves.

From Reality to Show

My mom and the other queens had encountered a formidable challenge: to communicate quickly, effectively, and memorably to unfamiliar receivers in an uncertain environment, first in terse writing, then in minute-long interpersonal interviews off-stage, then in brief broadcast interviews before a mass audience. They seemed keenly aware of their precarious journey through the elimination process: from the countless masses of women in the general population to only twenty whose written requests were right for the show; from twenty to four or five whose verbal expression, appearance, and manner were right; then to one with the ineffable qualities that enabled her to relate best to the audience, or masses, from which she had been scooped. Each step was an occasion to be rejected or chosen. It seems small wonder that the "queens" made much of their brief association with Hollywood celebrities, who struggle through a similar elimination process on a professional scale.

Within the elimination process, average women helped define acceptable broadcast communication practices, especially the earliest winners, as the show's format had not yet been thoroughly defined. The behavior of early contestants and audiences shaped both interviewing and voting practices. And to a certain extent, it established the producers' criteria for the selection of future candidates. Just as valuably, the women helped identify the characteristics and values of mainstream audiences and society in a changing world. For the most part, they made casual mention of the war, their displacement from home, and the country's steady transformation from agricultural to technological society, *seeming* to take the resulting strain and trauma in stride. The "villains" in their stories were usually medical maladies or other nonspecific calamities that struck randomly across classes and gender. According to the stories preferred by *Queen*, socioeconomic systems were in no way to blame for the plight of these women. What we mortals call "life" was to blame.

Queens offered entertaining performances that had served them well with friends and family in real life—they were well-mannered and they could make a good joke, share an endearing anecdote, or turn a lovely phrase. The nature of their requests did not always carry much weight. Their competence as ordinary conversationalists helped create an industry in which they shared no profits, but about which they seemed to share a rather proprietary attitude. Gradually, however, the tastes of producers and the requirements of commercial television became the principle factors in determining the worth of a woman's request.

As the show began to make more money, it became more heavily formatted and controlled, and the contestants lost most of their influence over broadcasting practices. Instead, they evidently adapted themselves to those practices as efficiently as possible. Steadily, people were altering the reality of their daily lives to fit the requirements of television. (Years later, these requirements would include a lack of civility unimaginable to the queens. The tagline of MTV's *Real World* was "When people stop being polite and start being real," as though politeness and reality could not coexist.)

Several queens stressed the importance of remaining upbeat in their neediness and emphasized the show's happy endings, which enhanced the message that life's never-ending crises could be routinely addressed and ameliorated through products. Everyday women may have appeared on the show seeking validation, but the show needed everyday women to maintain its own validation. In many ways, the experiences of queens functioned as a kind of microcosm and normalization of commercial broadcasting itself. Average people were allowed an evening in the company of celebrities, an escape from worry and drudgery, new and exotic experiences, excitement, romance, and probably most importantly, access to life-changing products. Spiritual transformation is invisible and therefore useless to television, but physical transformation not only can be shown, it can be sold.

Magic Merchandise and Magic Marketing

At one time, the economically deprived in Los Angeles, eager for the gospel message to the poor, filled the populist churches of evangelists such as "Fighting" Bob Schuler and Aimee Semple

McPherson. However, during the war and postwar years, as thousands of manufacturing jobs were created, folks drifted away from messages of the hereafter toward the marketed promise of heaven on earth, available now with our good credit. The next step was to demonstrate our overall worthiness to occupy this paradise of products.

Thus, real folks, "commoners," needed redefinition, and when the dust settled, some of us would be considered more common than others. Minorities, for example, were generally avoided as *Queen* contestants, as were extreme cases of any kind. One quickly scuttled request card read, "I want a gun." Nevertheless, a wide variety of contestants participated, providing a convincing appearance of equal access to the Californian dream. Not marginalized enough to be truly pathetic, the winners could be seen as ordinary people with extraordinary character.

Women in need often demonstrated an emotional attachment to the products they received from *Queen*, crying over a new dinette for example, and interestingly, these products did change women's lives and the lives of those around them. The products provided more than immediate relief from present difficulty—they often represented a fresh start in the world and hope for the future. Queens seemed most impressed by the fact that they were in fact *gifts*, unexpected and not requested. They just magically appeared.

Queen introduced the public to scores of new products, even as they were being developed. Their newness was itself attractive to several queens and may partially account for the "new life" the merchandise seemed to promise. Ingenious in its combination of needed items (the contestant's actual request) with luxury items (almost everything else she received), *Queen* revealed a basic practice in modern advertising that establishes a need for products when none exists and blurs the distinction between the necessary and the luxurious. We have routinely been encouraged to live like royalty.

Commercials "sell more than products, but a way of understanding the world."[11] Not all cultures have chosen to use television primarily to sell things, nor to dedicate to commercials the finest of its artistic talent. That we have done so has permanently affected the ways in which we make meaning of the world and ourselves as social actors. It also accounts for television's most relentless religious activity, evangelistic advertising.

The appeal of advertising must be understood in a cultural context in which the social status, employment, and even survival of people are separated from customary networks of skill and association. In a world of strangers, survival is to a large extent a matter of appearance and surface impressions.[12]

We can be saved through products. As small agricultural communities began to be replaced by urban manufacturing centers and then suburban housing and shopping centers, life became more mobile, less reliable, and peopled with strangers. Trademarks and brand names became the familiar, making people feel at home, and this familiarity became a bond between people who had little else in common.[13] Such relationships are reliant upon our view of ourselves "as a market, rather than a public, as consumers rather than citizens."[14] Products represent transcendence, lives transformed.[15]

Reality Advertising

One use of real people to naturalize mass culture is found in the authentic needs of competing queens and the often-traumatic content of their stories that lent dignity and weight far beyond their actual worth to mass-produced products. More important was the broadcast context of the women's true revelations, for the implication was that the mass audience, or community of strangers, had indeed replaced a local, personal community, and that members of this new mass community understood each other in terms of their shared consumerism. Television audiences replaced neighbors in determining one's likeability, sociability, and possible value to the community. TV provided solutions and support once offered by neighbors: help and comfort in time of need and illness.

However, unlike human neighbors, nothing was beyond the pale of television. Even a sick child's heart surgery was left up to the possibility that a TV show would save his or her life. True, one could still pray to God, but it was hard to count on so distant a supernatural being. TV could be up close and personal, and after all, it had pretty stunning sponsors. Wolcott Gibbs's wisecrack about "what God could do if only he had your money"[16] seemed to mirror the public's unspoken sentiment toward television.

A less obvious use of real people to naturalize market-driven culture could be found in broadcast emcees and announcers who appear(ed) genuine and likable, like the traveling salesmen in farming communities who needed to "sell themselves" through conversation and relationship-building before they could sell the products at hand.[17] *Queen* host, Jack Bailey, was a former carnival barker presumably well versed in the folksy, everyday interpersonal exchanges that folded easily into a basic principle of American marketing, "masking the ordinary in the dazzle of magic . . . and the lure of the unknown."

If American television has been designed to sell products, not only should TV personalities complement that end, so too should its programming genres.[18] Thus, the easily solved problems of situation comedies are complementary to the easily solved problems posed in commercials, the answers to which always lie in products. In order to enjoy a game show, we might need to share the goals of the contestant, and thus to value the prizes (products) for which they are competing. These goals and values have a religious flavor, since, again, products are meant to transform our lives. Over time it becomes less important that advertising complies with reality than that reality complies with advertising—a world of beautiful, shallow, sloganeering humans surrounded by shiny purchases.

The postwar decades of the *Queen* run were turbulent and unsettled, as are current times. During unsettled periods, "cultural meanings are more highly articulated and explicit, because they model patterns of action which do not 'come naturally.' "[19] In such a cultural context, the "available choices" presented by television (as well as *appearing* on television) cannot be underestimated. Such opportunities, representing more than the acquisition of merchandise, "determine which strategies, and thus which cultural [value] systems succeed."[20]

If participation in television offers opportunities that participation in everyday life does not, TV participation takes on a value of its own, (intensified by the exclusivity of such participation) regardless of how the individual "feels" about television. "In their ability to magnify, and to create near universal recognition, the mass media are able to invest the everyday lives of formerly everyday people with a magical sense of value, a secularized imprint of the sacred."[21]

Brushes with Greatness

Ancient Israel rejected the notion of a theocracy by asking God to give them a king so they could be like other nations. To this day, we want a monarch that looks and acts like us, only better; not the enormous deity beyond our reach, but a human sovereign that we might worship or topple at will. With the right stuff, one of us ordinary people might even become that sovereign. Ancient Egypt, with the aid of technology, built pyramids to usher mortals into immortality. We prefer television, and from it we pluck our own royalty from among our ranks: Elvis Presley, the "King of Rock and Roll," or the more obscure Mrs. Average American, "Queen for a Day." The word *queen* is an interesting choice in that it is a word commonly associated with wisdom, power, and influence. Yet no such attributes were assigned the winners on this show. Those connotations of *queen* were displaced by other meanings, such as "pampered" and "lucky." The enduring theme is power without responsibility.[22]

The experiences of queens resembled those of paid actors and other performers in Hollywood who, after a long day of work in the industry, returned to their everyday lives still wearing their stage makeup and costumes. Several queens were in fact employed by Hollywood (as dancers mostly), although they could not reveal this on the show. The implication was that one could not be truly average and be employed in show business, yet that was precisely the image of itself television was hoping to convey: an industry of real folks. Again, the historical context of early television was a contributing factor. In World War II, "the common man had conquered the world."[23] As a result, a common man was elected president. Our neighbors watched Eisenhower's inauguration in my mother's apartment because as elected Queen, she possessed the block's only television, "the post-war domestic appliance . . . standing in the corner of the living room . . . ready to unleash a new kind of American hero."[24]

The seeming commonness of the TV personality (Lucille Ball as opposed to Marilyn Monroe, Sid Caesar as opposed to Marlon Brando) was and is essential to the translation of everyday folk culture into marketed mass culture (or the actual into the artificial). Whereas the cinema had created stardom that was largely unattainable, TV made stardom possible and even natural. People such as the Queens for a Day became famous *because* of their everydayness, so long as it fit the purposes of television. The process worked both ways. Queen Elizabeth's real life coronation was available for viewing on television, which created "that unique cocktail of grandeur and coziness provided by squeezing the pageant into a box."[25] Thus, everyday women could be chosen to "reign" by design as Queen Elizabeth had been chosen by birth, sharing her celebrity/monarchy, with several of the same sacred implications.[26] The final lines of the Queen Club's "benediction" read: "To err is human, to forgive divine. To be divine is your task and mine."

Not much has changed. In a segment of *Extreme Makeover: Home Edition*, the home targeted for transformation was chosen because one of its residents had donated bone marrow used to restore an infant's life. That child was now three years old and her grateful mother nominated the donor as a candidate for a new home. With a one-week deadline contrived to heighten suspense, the team went to work, gleefully destroying the family's existing home and creating another directly out of designs in ideal home magazines and ads. Along the way, the crew found time to give blood on the set, reminding viewers to do the same at their local blood banks.

Celebrities from a football team admired by the family's youngest boy stopped by to offer helmets that were used as bed posts. Amid the general feeling of an old fashioned barn raising, with millions of unseen dollars and stop camera technology that made the crew's efforts invisible and magical, a two story house complete with swimming pool suddenly appeared in a working class neighborhood of a downbeat San Bernardino suburb. There, back-dropped by the new Jacuzzi, patio furniture, and manicured landscaping, the bone marrow recipient and her tearful mother were introduced to the lifesaving new home owner. One of the crew told the camera that this particular episode involved "not a design intervention, but a divine intervention."

The Greek word for church, *ecclesia*, literally means "called out ones." Airwaves seem to call us out from everyday life in a similar way, and to reward us for lives well lived.[27] But there is an important, sneaky difference between being a survivor (to reference another reality show) and being saved. Survival has more to do with the Darwinism pushed by television and, for that matter, by a church that chooses to prove its anti-Darwinism via Darwinist principles; the ichthys devouring the "Darwin fish" on victorious car bumpers.

David Brooks tells us that through higher education, we have replaced a social structure of aristocracy with one of "meritocracy," in which individuals earn their right to rule, so to speak.[28] In California, television has enabled us to do the same. Cal-types are raised to believe that through extraordinary talent or personality, any and every person can *merit* success, and that success runs the gamut from mere survival to fame, fortune, and semidivinity, though sometimes these all appear to be intermingled. It may be difficult for the successful to imagine the need for salvation, or for a gospel of grace to make sense in our local star system. Difficult, but not impossible.

5

Who Is My Neighbor?

Sociology and Politics

On a Sunday when I was around seven, my hair still combed so tightly it gave me a headache, I was once again staring down at my organza dress with little purple flowers on a white background, trying hard to reach that safe little world far from the Inland Empire. My siblings and I were sitting in the backseat of my father's Desoto on the way home from church, listening to him scream at my mom. He had taken a rare blend of prescription drugs that had made him unusually crazy, and he was driving erratically toward the cemetery, then into a vacant lot that served as a dumping ground for dead floral bouquets and such. With his right hand, he was hitting my mom.

"You kids are going to get to watch me kill your mother!" he shouted, as I tried to push my back clear through the seat and disappear into the upholstery. He lurched to a stop and pushed my mother out of the car. Her torn skirt was falling toward her ankles and making her stumble as she began to run uphill. She was praying out loud as my dad drove the car toward her, and just as the bumper touched her, the engine died.

My mom kept running, to the first house she found, and pounded at the door. She expected to face strangers and tried to compose herself so she wouldn't scare them. The man who answered recognized her as the nurse who had cared for his mother and quickly agreed to help. When he and my mom arrived back at the Desoto, I thought I was seeing things. "Having car trouble, buddy?" he calmly asked my father. Dad nodded. "Well, I think I might be able to take a look at the engine, but tell you what. Why don't I take your wife and kids home first?" Dad nodded again. "Thanks."

We ended up at my grandparents' house, where we usually went after such episodes with my dad. Hours later, my grandma urged my mom to come along to the evening church service, as a pageant play was being performed that would surely make her feel better. My mom resisted, naturally. Her eye had been blackened and her hair pulled away from part of her scalp. But my grandma convinced her that she could wear a scarf far enough forward to hide both injuries, and that she might make an early exit to avoid being seen. So that night we sat in a pew at the back of the church and watched as the lights came up on stage to reveal a tableau of the angel Gabriel addressing Mary at the annunciation. My father was playing the angel.

I'm convinced God saved my mother's life that day and that a neighbor provided the rescue and relief that our church could not. "Good news to the poor" could only be received from a willing helper, not from an outstanding performer. There's nothing very flashy about helping others, and personal involvement runs the risk of toil and time-consumption Cal-types simply cannot afford. Furthermore, what if we don't like our neighbor? What if our neighbor is undeserving or ungrateful? To Christ's mandate that we love one another as he has loved us, we have often responded, "Sorry. This empire-building is a full time job."

In the empire, we attempt to dazzle God with our own spirituality, just enough to convince God to bless us. Scriptural evidence to the contrary, the assumption here is that God's blessings rely on our character, rather than God's, and that's enough to panic anybody. It probably goes without saying that life on this spiritual treadmill can have disastrous social consequences on relationships of every kind. We may not know our own families, let alone our neighbors, but that won't stop us from making demands of both. If the land isn't good enough, and we're not good enough, and the *gospel* isn't good enough, well then, our neighbors surely won't be good enough.

F. Scott Fitzgerald understood this relentless longing and dissatisfaction as an American trait. But if Gatsby was murdered in the East, he made a stunning recovery in the West, and has been throwing wild parties ever since. According to one historian, Fitzgerald's Californian counterpart, John Steinbeck, "provides an acute analysis of the national equation of the movement West with the pursuit of an endless desire, a desire valuable precisely because it cannot be fulfilled and therefore one at war with the domestic."[1] In such an environment, hospitality is one of the first things to go, no matter how many guests may be invited. Gatsby rarely tries to converse with his guests, only to impress them. His parties are based on consumption, not friendship.

The Guest List

California's gold rush produced an international community overnight. Our state's diversity has afforded us an opportunity largely unavailable to the rest of the nation: the chance to create a multiethnic setting that enriches us all, to address the subsequent challenges with grace, and to emerge from the task with helpful recommendations for those regions whose diversity comes less naturally. In our best moments, California has made many, many such attempts, often with laudable success. But we have also, on occasion, adjusted ourselves to the nation's worst biases.

"An article on immigration in the distinguished literary journal *Overland Monthly* confessed to readers that 'San Francisco is not an American city.' For Americans in the East, San Francisco's ethnic diversity was undoubtedly one of its most characteristic features, and one that raised serious questions about its long-term stability. State boosters would attempt to turn this liability into an asset by showing foreigners as both hardworking and picturesque."[2] The Cal-type still prefers that our immigrants be hardworking and picturesque, a difficult combination of qualities that we citizens may or may not possess ourselves. Thus, "a mystique of invitation has traditionally operated . . . to mask a stubbornly recurring politics of exclusion."[3]

According to author Claire Perry, "Promotional images during the latter part of the [nineteenth] century showed that California's bounty was available to the American Everyman, or at least to those with enough cash for a down payment."[4] One widely distributed promotional text screamed, "CALIFORNIA . . . The Cornucopia of the World . . . Room for millions of Immigrants . . . 43,795,000 Acres of Government Lands Untaken . . . Railroad and Private Land for a Million Farmers . . . A Climate for Health and Wealth without Cyclones or Blizzards."[5] Unfortunately, a different kind of cyclone awaited, for our diversity resulted in "collision rather than community."[6]

David Wyatt observes, "The emerging myth of the California frontier—a myth of the freedom and the purity of the national character—veiled a struggle over race and gender. Although the myth served to invite everyone in, the politics on the ground proceeded with relocations, exclusions, and scapegoatings."[7] The shameful, routinely lawless power grabs that created a "California of broken contracts and sudden carnage"[8] have affected California Indians, Mexicans, Chinese, Japanese, African Americans, and numberless other ethnicities in their turn, with female populations within these groups faring worst of all.

Benjamin C. Truman, author of various railroad-sponsored tracts, "gave the rallying cry of the more aggressive approach to immigration: 'Look this way, ye seekers after home and happiness!' he called. 'Ye honest sons of toil and ye *pauvres miserables* who are dragging out a horrible life in the purlieus of Eastern cities! Semi-Tropical California welcomes you all.' "[9] But these *pauvres miserables*, like the "tired, the poor, the huddled masses yearning to be free" landing in New York's harbor, would find their welcome a highly conditional one.

"At the same time that California attracted immigrants with a dream of home ownership, a good job, and a place in the sun, it indentured many of them into an economy precariously based on growth and bigness."[10] What the gold rush started the post–World War II boom perfected one hundred years later. "Ten percent of all federal monies during the war were spent in California, an influx of capital that established the nation's largest military–industrial complex."[11] The defense industry created a 72.2 percent growth in migration during the 1940s alone and a brand new population easily as diverse as that surrounding the gold rush. For a while, home ownership flourished among this diverse population, along with opportunities in education and business. But by the time I was walking home from school with my friends, I could hear conservative journalist George Putnam's daily televised tirade against the many threats posed by such a population.

The distrust that led to the appalling relocation of Japanese Americans during the war was turned upon neighbor after neighbor.[12] "Los Angeles hurt me racially as much as any city I have ever known—much more than any city I remember from the South," wrote a friend of Langston Hughes in 1945.[13] Combined with the many other "anxieties of abundance"[14] that once again created high stakes, fearful self-interest led to "the repeal of the Rumford Fair Housing Act by two-thirds of California voters in 1964—the beginning of a swing to the right in California politics that would lead to the election of Ronald Reagan as governor in 1966 and the property tax revolts of the 1970s."[15] That swing would have lasting consequences for education. But Californians could not look out for others because everyone's own wealth was precarious, teetering upon a defense industry based on apprehensive images of unseen enemies.

My Space

True to gold rush form, the Cal-type is still looking out for number one, still staking claims, corporately and individually, whether in traffic jams or grocery lines or crowded gyms or sales bins or church pews. We're still eyeing our neighbor suspiciously, still on guard against the foreign element, which can be anyone that threatens our space. The overnight explosion of MySpace users from two to two million was not at all astonishing if one lived in California. MySpace and subsequent social networking sites allow us to claim a spot on the Internet and communicate virtually with others, giving us the power to deny communication as well, instantly and openly, without any of those awkward moments that might arise in real, physical human encounters.

Such sites provide a way to both evaluate others and to be evaluated by them, and if there's one thing we're getting down well, it's the evaluation process. In 1993, Neil Postman warned Americans that the IQ Test would lead to any number of devices inappropriately designed to measure ineffable human qualities.[16] Sure enough, we blithely proceeded beyond Postman's wildest protests into the arms of countless experts, legitimate or otherwise. They gave us grid after grid by which to rate one another efficiently and unapologetically, often leading to some judgment that may in fact have deadly consequences. While we can laugh at the judges on American Idol who instruct the public on how to evaluate talent, we might easily overlook the ways in which the rest of us, in our everyday lives, are "voting people off the show" or "off the island," a la *Survivor*.

The response of *Survivor* producers to criticism that the show lacked ethnic diversity says it all. The fall 2006 season of *Survivor* actually would divide its twenty contestants into four different teams based on race. Said host Jeff Probst, "I think it fits in perfectly with what *Survivor* does—it is a social experiment."[17] Perhaps Probst doesn't know that a social experiment on race has been going on for some time, in the far more vital realms of politics, education, economics, and inevitably, religion.

Through early immigration practices, Californians literally voted people off the island by creating unreachable standards. "Immigrants arriving at Ellis Island in New York were asked, typically, twenty-nine questions; at Angel Island [California] those seeking entry could be asked from two hundred to one thousand."[18] The No Child Left Behind educational program can tend to have much the same effect on California's immigrant population. Since children who are still struggling with the language and other obstacles are evaluated on the same grid as everyone else, when they fail, they are punished along with their teachers and their schools via reduced funding. Thus it becomes more important to pass the evaluation than to acquire needed knowledge, more important to appear to be learning than to actually learn.

A few years ago my sister, a longtime grammar school teacher in La Puente District, asked her class to solve a verbal math problem involving the number of liters it would take to fill a bathtub. One student stared back at her and she reviewed the equation formula. The student continued to stare. "What don't you understand?" she asked. "What's a bathtub?" the child replied. My sister turned to the rest of the room. "How many of you don't know what a bathtub is?" Several children raised their hands, even though they had been trying to work out the problem.

Surely, one major issue affecting immigration policy in California lies in our unreconciled past with Mexico. Not only did we refuse to recognize the native inhabitants of California as having rightful domain, we disregarded the claims of another established government. When people ask film director Luis Valdez what part of Mexico he comes from, he jokes, "California." Yet unlike Texas, where the United States forcibly annexed Mexican territory, we don't quite remember our Alamo. Today, many seem to believe that Spanish translations of public documents in California are the result of some sort of public handout, when in fact they are one of Mexico's reasonable terms of concession. When we've addressed "the Mexican problem" in California, we've been prone to pass anti-immigrant propositions while munching popcorn and watching *Zorro* survive insurmountable odds on the movie screen.

This reflects an old relationship with the "hard-working, picturesque" Mexican, who was exploited for labor and exotic image while being criticized and marginalized for both. "After

1869," in order to invigorate the gold-depleted land, "pictures that described the stately pace of mission life and the gay abandon of the *rancho* days nurtured the idea that a graciousness long absent from the lives of wage earners in the East was still present in California."[19] This lay in stark contrast to "the vehemence of the American contempt for Mexican Californians conveyed in the account of the Yankee trapper James Clyman, who toured the territory during the 1840s. Clyman dismissed his hosts as 'a thieving, cowardly, dancing, lewd people,' who, furthermore, were also 'generally indolent and faithless.' "[20]

Far from enjoying their neighbors' "gracious living" patterns, "newcomers from the East were afraid that, by living among the Mexican Americans, they might become infected by the endemic laziness that Richard Henry Dana had called the 'California Fever.' " During the gold rush, a series of statutes and taxes were enacted "to prevent 'greasers' from competing with [Yankees] in the mines."[21] Part of the efforts to re-create the communities and institutions Anglos had left behind in the East included erasing all evidence of the Latin way of life, so that "by the end of the 1860s, many significant aspects of Spanish culture had been effectively neutralized, including the *rancho* system, the remnants of mission culture, and the influence of important Mexican-American families."[22]

Once these had been eliminated as a threat, they could be renegotiated, hence celebrated. The diligent campaign to scrub away the traces of California's Spanish past during the 1850s and 1860s, as well as the exuberant Hispanophilia of the later decades of the century, act as a testament to the tenacious adaptability of the state's business leaders. California's Old World heritage suddenly represented, rather than a burden and an embarrassment, a potentially lucrative tourist attraction. Those who had been the most energetic critics of the state's Hispanic residents now became enthusiastic boosters for Spanish California, promoting the venerable missions, the quaint remnants of Mexican *pueblos*, and the colorful traditions of California's Spanish-speaking population as cherished features of the state's cultural assets.[23]

The problem, of course, is that real live people don't behave like those in our imaginations. When my daughter was four years old, she had imaginary friends. One day when I entered her room she was standing on her bed, hands on hips, saying to them, "Look, I made you all up and I can get rid of you any time I want!" She outgrew this stage in her life. Would that were true for all of us. An imaginary friendship with Mexico has often been based on whimsy or self-interest. It has even been forced, as it was by the "Good Neighbor Policy" the federal government imposed during World War II. But true neighborliness can only be demonstrated when real people are involved.

Home Dis-associations

A homeowner's association is created by a real estate developer to manage a certain housing development and then transferred to the homeowners in that development once the homes have been sold. The association manages the development (that which we once might have called "the neighborhood") as a sort of nonprofit corporation to which dues are paid and from which benefits may be derived. One function of the association is to set and enforce standards of home design and maintenance, and even a homeowner's behavior on occasion.

One of the disturbing implications of the homeowner's association is that it provides yet one more means to police our neighbors rather than interact with them. The home as individual investment property can so easily take precedence over all other concerns, given the high cost of ownership. Our neighbors can become just one more feature on the real estate flier, like the swimming pool or the spacious garage. Are the neighbors an attractive feature or not? Thus, neighbors are held to the standards, albeit self-imposed, of the association. If they break the rules, it is easier to report our neighbors to the association than to speak to them, much less understand or accommodate them.

It seems to me this personal policy eventually finds its way into public policy, whereby lawsuits replace dialogue. In the absence of a shared moral code, in an environment where it's every man for himself, California-ism can easily become less concerned with what is right than with what is *legal*. The Cal-type's job becomes to compile a list of justifiable grievances against our neighbors, especially those who remain strangers to us. Let's get them fined, get them punished, get them thrown out. And on and on, until, by the time we reach California's penal system, this attitude has morphed into the Three Strikes Law, whereby a relatively short list of certain crimes can imprison a neighbor permanently. Proponents of this law have made sound and convincing arguments, I know. But, again, my concern is that "Three Strikes and You're Out" represents a more general thought pattern.

Sadly, much of the time we're kept too busy evaluating the behavior of our neighbors to address the needs of our neighbors. California-ism is quick to identify the undeserving poor, as George Bernard Shaw puts it in *Pygmalion*, but not so quick to identify the deserving poor. Are they the hardworking poor? Not really, for we refuse day laborers admission to our hospitals. Are they the enterprising poor? Not really, for we deny self-sustaining farmers access to their land. Are they the sober poor? Not really, for we cancel food programs to toddlers. Are they the pitiable poor? Not really, because we fail to shelter the elderly and infirm. They *are*, it seems, the lucky poor, those that make the cut in our arbitrary man-made systems. During the gold rush, " 'luck' became the dominant metaphor for agency,"[24] and I believe it still is.

I hear my little neighbor's voice as she chases the ice cream truck. "Whoa!" she cries. "Wait! I'm coming! Please, wait!" and in her panting and pleading I hear the ongoing cries of so many Californians who have scraped together the price of their hoped-for purchase—a car or a house or a business—too late. You're out of luck. Speculation has rocked real estate, loaning, and every related cost, placing so much just outside the reach of struggling families or even middle-class ones. The enterprise has moved on to others who may be lucky enough to seize whatever beguiling opportunity the state still offers. Their luck will itself be considered a sign of God's blessing, God's blessing a sign of their worthiness, and so on, as it was from the beginning. There is nothing very new and even less very interesting about this attitude. Christ encountered it repeatedly. His own disciples were astonished by his assertion that the rich were not innately better people than the poor, although he kept trying to convince them of its truth.

The gubernatorial election of the lucky immigrant Arnold Schwarzenegger in the California recall election is worth noting. A friend from the East telephoned me shortly after Schwarzenegger's election to ask what I thought about it, and I replied that I thought it proved to the rest of the country that California was just about as unsteady as they thought it was. Schwarzenegger is a likeable guy and, as I've noted, could end up being a respectable governor. But that may be beside the point. The very fact that we are one of the only states in the union with a recall process says something about how we conduct political life. No one's leadership position is safe, and in a way, this is an unusually democratic and progressive setup. However, the possibility always exists that we will recall a leader not for ordinary incompetence, but, rather, as in the case of Grey Davis, for extraordinary unluckiness. The Cal-type prefers to be governed by a celebrity without legislative experience but with proven luck.

Schwarzenegger's predecessor Ronald Reagan was not the first lucky celebrity whose political career was launched in California. Before that came George Murphy. The charming ways of these movie stars were even less important than their seemingly charmed lives, and the fact that none of them seemed to be uncommonly talented actors only enhanced our faith in their lucky breaks. References to luck were built into the language of Schwarzenegger's political speeches. And yet, this brand of luck subtly dissolves into a sort of reward for one's faith—not necessarily faith in God, but faith in the American way, which increasingly has become equated with chauvinism, privatization, and corporateering.

Along the metaphoric way, little acknowledgment is made of favors that we have received or mercies we have been shown.

Suddenly, we are a state populated by self-made men, whose granddad immigrated here too but by damn, he learned to speak English, and by damn, he worked his way through the system without any handouts, and by damn, so can *these* people. As though it were possible that we or our forebears were never recipients of any form of grace. Only in "this culture of transience and amnesia"[25] does such an assumption seem possible.

Culture Crash

My husband and I recommended the academy-award-winning film *Crash* to friends who were relatively new to California. When I asked them how they liked it, they confessed that they were really disappointed. They had expected a sensitive portrayal of race relations, and instead confronted characters as stereotypical as those in any racist film. I told them I believed that was because *Crash* is not really so much a movie about racial issues, as it is about Los Angeles. In Los Angeles, image, ethnic and otherwise, is usually all we know of one another, and most of these images are drawn straight from central casting. In a city held so firmly in the grip of mass media, "illusion rivals economic disparity as an enemy to peace. The cultural machine that produces images of difference, and the discontent they breed, works faster and more efficiently than the political or economic system can work to eliminate actual material difference."[26]

Other urban areas have distinct ethnic neighborhoods, but they also have distinct city centers and a relatively heavy reliance upon public transit. Folks (until recently, anyway) had to travel through neighborhoods other than their own, unwillingly perhaps, and warily, but nonetheless with some dim awareness of their genuine, living "neighbors." Not so here. Directly from our homes and gated communities, we enter our autos or SUVs (gated communities on wheels) and head for the freeway on-ramps and off-ramps, to our places of business, without ever seeing a neighborhood of any kind.[27] Thus, about the only images we have of our neighbors are the ones we draw from the media, and those images are themselves, ironically, produced by our local media industry. In actuality, we have little to do with one another until we collide.[28]

This, then, is the central point of *Crash*, which comments upon ethnic misrepresentation via the film's style as well as its content. I believe this is why all the characters take the form of stereotypes and then, trapped in their stereotypical representations, attempt to negotiate their way through an incumbent series of racial encounters, or "accidents." Not only do the characters of *Crash* not know their neighbors in Los Angeles, in the words of one young Latina in the film, they need "a geography lesson" about their neighbors worldwide. None are able to distinguish between who is Mexican and who is from another Latin American country, and there seems to be no felt need to know anything more about the area than that "everyone parks their car on the lawn." In other scenes, a Persian family is mistaken first as Iraqi, then as Arab, and mistreated on both occasions.

The film's opening lines belong to Don Cheadle as police detective Graham Waters, who has just survived a car accident. "In L.A., nobody touches you. Everyone's behind metal and glass. We miss touch so much we crash into each other." Graham leaves the car and approaches another investigator who is examining another accident victim. "What d'ya got?" He asks. "Dead kid," comes the reply. This nameless kid will turn out to be Waters's missing brother, Peter, whom their mother has asked him to protect. Graham has not been able to find his brother and we will soon learn he hasn't been looking very hard.

Instead, he tries to protect Peter by bending the law in backroom deals. Significantly, his brother is teetering on the final of three strikes and risks being put away permanently. Consequently, Waters is so busy expunging his brother's criminal record (symbolically, the kinds of records we all keep on one another, at varying levels) that he cannot do the one thing he really needs to do: find his brother and save his life. But finding and saving are exactly the goals of Christ.[29] Scripture asks us to feed the poor, to which we are tempted to respond, sure, if they'll go to church and behave themselves; in other words, when they have a clean record.

In *Crash*, whenever life is threatened, it is because a human evaluation has been made. Whenever life is saved, it is the result of a supernatural act of grace that makes use of human agency without reliance on human evaluations. The Persian shop owner, Farhad, will attempt to kill Daniel, the Mexican locksmith, but Farhad's daughter will indirectly preserve life and protect father and victim. Later, Farhad will credit his unseen angel for this miracle and Daniel will credit the faith of his own little girl. Both will be changed by their metaphysical encounter of grace, but neither will have done anything to deserve it.

Astutely, *Crash* explores the issues of law and grace by grounding its story in the literal (if corrupt) law, the LAPD. Matt Dillon's character, Officer John Ryan, is the "bad cop" to Ryan Phillippe's "good cop," Officer Hanson. Officer Ryan's misplaced anger over an unjust systemic problem (the insurance company denying his father coverage) is rerouted into a personal problem with the company's representative, Shaniqua, an African American that he evaluates as undeserving of her position. In turn, Shaniqua won't save the life of Ryan's father because she has evaluated Ryan's behavior as undeserving.

In Ryan's simmering rage, he spies Cameron, an African American television producer driving "too nice" a car in "too nice" a neighborhood,[30] and without provocation, pulls him over and molests his wife, humiliating both during a "routine search" for drugs. His partner is disgusted by this outright display of racism, and asks his African American police chief for a transfer. The chief, whose office displays a large glossy of Arnold Schwarzenegger, refuses to report the incident and to openly acknowledge the systemic problem of racism in the LAPD. The chief is performing well in that system and being rewarded. So he tells Officer Hanson he should "admit to having an embarrassing [bodily] problem of a personal nature" in order to escape partnership with officer Ryan.[31]

Elsewhere in Los Angeles, Anthony, played by rapper Ludacris, and Peter are two young African Americans "living up to their stereotype," as the District Attorney implies, by hijacking automobiles, one of which belongs to Cameron. Cameron is furious with Peter, and as he scolds him, the car begins to weave. As a result of this hijacking, and the hasty, misguided judgment of the LAPD who should have been protecting him, Cameron is pulled over in a cul-de-sac and held at gunpoint. The injustices of the previous twenty-four hours overwhelm him and in his hopelessness, he behaves recklessly. Officer Hanson tries to rescue him while defending the system. "They want to shoot you, and the way you're acting, it would be completely justified," Hanson claims, adding, "I'm trying to help you." This is not the kind of help Cameron wants. He does not want to be "forgiven" by a faulty system, forgiven for the contrived crime of being African American. He wants a different system.

It's the System, I Tell Ya'

God has a different system. God's system does not squeeze itself into our puny notions of "just deserts." God's favor cannot be merited by anyone and is available to everyone, because it rests on God's character, not ours. We sort of hate this, so we cling to our own miserable system, a system we think we can beat through our fine behavior, pious preaching, and winning performances. "You think you're better than me? You judge me?" Ryan asks Hanson. "You think you know who you are. You have no idea." There's no escaping the system because the system is sin itself, from which Christ alone can free. Therefore, it is deeply meaningful that when random acts of grace occur in *Crash*, they are always miraculous. We look at such supernatural acts as glitches in our system, but in reality, these are hints of God's system, invading our system against our expectations.

Like Hanson, we are inclined to do our favors with the expectation of gratitude that will then change the behavior of the recipient. But shockingly, Christ saves us regardless of whether or not our gratitude changes our behavior. It will, of course; but if our system is focused on making people better behaved, Christ's "system" is based on saving their lives. A woman who must be pulled from the car that will catch fire at any moment is the same woman Ryan has molested the previous evening. But now he isn't cruising around town with the luxury of evaluating and humiliating his neighbor. He cannot act out of his loathsome prejudice (literally, pre-judgment) if he is to act in grace.

In this respect, grace is unreasonable. The concept itself is beyond human reason because we ourselves are not gracious by nature. This is why Hanson, responding with fearful instincts, will later murder Waters's brother, Peter, after doing him the favor of giving him a ride. When we act according to our own notions of grace, we will quickly reach our limit, because we're not truly acting in grace at all. Only God is truly gracious and when God shows us how dire the human situation really is, we are forced to act against our "better judgment" and take risks. In Ryan's situation, this takes the form of emotional risk as well as physical, for there is no guarantee that the wronged woman will trust him to help her.

It is always thus when we truly serve our neighbors. We are always acting against the "better judgment" that looks out for our own interests, as the criminal Anthony does when he later releases the Asian refugees trapped in the back of a stolen van and nearly sold into slavery. He is acting graciously *despite* his character, not because of it. He's still part of the system. "This is America. Time is money! Chop, chop!" he hollers. Yet miraculously, grace intervenes and lives are saved, even though Anthony's parting words are "Dopey, f-----n' Chinaman."

There is much name-calling in *Crash*, but few know their neighbors' actual names. What makes the Cal-type dangerous is not that we don't know our neighbors, but that we think we do. Moreover, we confuse tolerating our neighbor with loving our neighbor. Upon winning the 1996 Independent Spirit Award, Sean Penn declared, "I guess this means you tolerate me, you really tolerate me!" People know when we are being tolerated, and it is a lonely, deadening sensation. In *Crash*, Graham Waters tolerates his brother instead of loving him, and it ends in his brother's death. Waters tolerates his mother, the backsliding junkie, who weeps to him "I was doing good. I was doing real good." She will attribute Waters's tolerant act of kindness in buying her groceries to his wayward but loving brother. As in Christ's parable of the prodigal son, there is no mention of the good son or the bad son in this story, only the living son and the dead son. "Did you find your brother?" she asks Waters repeatedly. It is the same question God asks us. "Tell him to come home," the mother adds.

When I lived in Kentucky, I remember telling a friend that I could never settle there because California was my home. "Why does that sound funny to me?" she drawled. Despite our image as vacation resort to the world, California has indeed become home to much of the world, whether or not anyone's "better judgment" would have it that way. The welcome we offer to others, like the welcome the Statue of Liberty offers immigrants to America, may from time to time only be the welcome to serve or spend, not to live. "Welcome to California," snaps a bumper sticker. "Now go home." But what if this is our home?

In *Crash*, Hanson orders Cameron to go home and he quickly replies, "Yeah. *That* I can do." Home is a safe haven that does not exist in the larger community. In the eighties, Margaret Thatcher declared, "There is no such thing as society. There are only individuals and their families." It sounded outrageous to me at the time, but we seem to have proceeded as though we believed that. It has left many of us with a sense of loss and maybe even occasional panic, something like the DA's wife in *Crash*, who confides, "I wake up like this every morning. I feel angry all the time and I don't know why. I don't know why." Her home can never be made safe enough or clean enough to calm her.

Maybe because so few of us really feel at home here, there is a lack of hospitality to others.[32] But without the sense that we are sharing the same home, we can never know our neighbors, let alone love them. When my son was very little, he used to take a chair out to our front lawn and sit there like an old man, waving to passing traffic. At Christmastime, he carried a large songbook out with him and loudly sang to the cars "Deck the halls with balls of jolly," undaunted by the whizzing barricades of metal and glass. These were his neighbors.

In the final scenes of *Crash*, we discover that Peter and Hanson have something in common, something that is a source of ironic connection to one and fearful distancing to the other. They both carry little statues of St. Christopher, the patron saint of travelers. Hanson has tried to offer hospitality in the form of a ride to the stranded Peter, but neither of them is ever at home, so not only is hospitality impossible, but their shared fate as travelers gets Peter killed. Later, Cameron is traveling when he notices the miraculous snow falling on the car Hanson burns to hide his criminal act, rather than confessing. Halted by the image, Cameron glances down at his cell phone and sees another kind of miracle in Los Angeles, "Home calling."

Los Neighbors

Following a play we attended at the Mark Taper Forum, my husband and I walked through the outer courtyard of the Music Center where the City of Los Angeles was sponsoring an outdoor dance. Wonderful Latin music was playing and the area was jammed with dancers of every possible hue. Some danced well and some badly, but all danced joyfully. By and by, a police helicopter came overhead and hovered there spewing fumes and searchlights. The crowd gazed up at the helicopter without alarm, laughing and waving. It went away and we cheered. As the band played its final number, the leader thanked us for coming and dancing. "Everyone," he shouted, "regardless of our race or nationality, we are all just people together, right? Never forget that!" Then he introduced the band. They called themselves Los Neighbors. My husband gave me a final twirl and I bumped into the dancer next to me. But we didn't crash.

6

The Mastered Race

Celebrity Culture

One of California's most famous attempts at advertising this lush state remains the Pasadena Rose Parade, which shows the world that even in the dead of winter, New Year's Day, flowers grow here so plentifully that we can cover entire floats with them. During the Rose Parade coverage of 2005, television host Bob Eubanks explained that the reason Pasadena had long ago decided not to conduct the parades on Sunday was because the floats startled the horses of churchgoers. Observing that the parade had enjoyed clear skies ever since, Eubanks concluded, "We have a deal with God: I won't rain on your parade if you won't hold it on Sundays."[1]

The following year, a torrential storm hit the parade. Those who endured were whipped by winds and soaked through with rain, even though the officials dutifully skipped Sunday and held the parade Monday, January 2. Why won't God live up to our imaginary bargains? Evidently, God will do what God will do and those folks who stayed in the most punishing parade of recent history are the ones with real stories to tell, not because they impressed God, but because they have been impressed *by* God. Perhaps they have even been changed by this memorable event. However, history indicates that more often than not, we'd rather change God than change ourselves.

The replacement of the real God with a preferred god is automatic to humans. Both John Calvin and Martin Luther noted that the human heart is a natural idol maker. So natural is this behavior that the very first commandment delivered to Moses on Mount Sinai forbids it. Theologian Richard Keyes has observed that the real God is impossible to grasp because by nature God is *both* personal (nearby) *and* all-powerful (far off) and we simply cannot take that in. Thus our more shallow preference is to sort of split God in half and create our own nearby, accessible gods to provide us with the hopes offered by our own far-off gods. If we make them up, chances are we can understand—and control—them better.[2]

Here's how it works. Let's assume my longing is for the far-off "god" of eternal life, but I don't trust the real God to get the job done. Well, then, I will worship the nearby god (for example, fame or physical perfection) so that either my name or my image will endure forever. Or, let's assume my nearby god is security but I don't trust the real God to take care of me. Then my nearby god might become wealth or influence, and plenty of it, so I can take care of myself no matter what. In a nutshell, we should be able to tell what our nearby gods are by one simple test. They are those things to which we make sacrifices.

It's the System, Man

The Hollywood star system was carefully manufactured in the early years of the film industry.[3] Lining the boulevards of Hollywood with banners depicting images of certain actors, initiating glamour magazines to enlarge their lives, staging special events to insure public attendance: these were activities that began in the 1910s. The star system was initiated for economic reasons, not cultural ones. If Hollywood had not created the star system, surely we would have created something else to serve the same purposes in our lives. But as it stands, when it comes to make-it-yourself divinity, this system really does promise it all. All the usual far-off gods of our impoverished imaginations are represented (fame, wealth, power, etc.), yet the stars are so nearby. In fact, they are *Us*, they are *People*, as the popular magazine titles imply.

Like the gods of Greek mythology, the stars have all the longings of humans, but the clout to do something about it. And like the people of ancient Athens, those of us in California tell the Macedonians (that is, the rest of the world), "We have heard the thunderbolts of the gods!" At the screening of the short-lived film *Troy*, I can't have been the only one in the audience who squirmed in my seat as Brad Pitt, playing Achilles, sighed about the terrible problems of being considered both god and man.

Actors have been associated with spiritual activity from the dawn of Western civilization, inasmuch as they acted in Greek and Roman theater that was itself the very site of worship. In fact, the early church would not allow actors to join them because it was assumed that if someone was an actor, that person already had a religion. What we may fail to notice is how much religious activity is still taking place at the theater.[4] And what we may like best about this setup is that we ourselves become omniscient and omnipresent when we watch a movie.

Sitting in the hushed darkness of the film cathedral, enjoying our sacramental popcorn for which we've paid too high a price, congregants gaze at the altar of the screen and are given plot information that many characters in the movie do not know and cannot control. We piece together the story we are told, traveling from location to location with or without all the characters, filling in the narrative gaps, and thus it begins to feel as though we ourselves are telling the story. It seems to be our own idea, and thus difficult to refute for the time being, whether or not it aligns with our general beliefs.

Needless to say, in keeping with empire precedent, the film and recording industries contain powerful enough technologies to insure the success of this mystical enterprise. The movie screen that makes humans larger than life, yet draws audiences into intimacy that is not possible in normal theatrical environments, the soundtrack that touches our spirit as nothing else can, the camera, lighting, editing, and special effects, all these lend a supernatural component to the action and serve to make the narrative seem at least as vital as the one we're hearing at church.

Importantly, these are often the narratives that are defining good and evil, especially if they are those of the American action film, a time-honored arena of American moral reasoning that doggedly submits to the conventions of classical Hollywood cinema. It positions a lone hero—most often a beleaguered, likable common man of uncommon character and inner strength—within a larger-than-life struggle between good and evil in which evil is overcome temporarily, until the next action film. At that time the same process (the same ritual) will be repeated with a new villain. In this way, the audience is capable of redefining morality along the lines of contemporary cultural biases concerning both our current enemies and how best to defeat them.

This process is of particular importance to a democratic nation in which every person is expected to perform the duties formerly placed upon the shoulders of monarchs (that is, to create public policy, elect leadership, and pass judgment upon others via the jury process). Monarchy had the advantage of being considered God's choice, invested by divine right to make such decisions. However, without such an assumption of the sacred in our midst, it becomes the American public's duty to identify the slippery boundaries of good and evil.[5] This we often do in collaboration with the heady powers of the silver screen and its partner melodrama, which together comprise the very seat of public moral argument.

What Do You Mean, Nobody's Perfect?

In blending the power of actors with the power of gods we have concocted quite a potent spiritual brew. Of course, given the

Cal-type's dim attitude toward the gospel of grace, and true to the "new models of rebellion and control" that might substitute for that gospel, these gods of our own making must earn our worship. Ancient peoples fed their idols (as we do with box office receipts) and dressed up their idols (as we do with fashion magazines) when they were happy with them. They also spanked their idols (as we do with gossip magazines) when they were unhappy. We, like they, rarely let our idols out of our sight, nor stop making unreasonable demands of them.

Greek worshipers expected to meet their gods in person at the temple, as we meet ours at the movie theater or in magazines. Thus life-sized statues had to be created, not just small figurines. Soon the Greeks were dissatisfied with realistic depictions of humans. They were capable of realism, but instinctively avoided it in their art, just as we often do now. Realism is not often considered beautiful enough, no matter how beautiful, so sculptors created abnormally developed shoulders, chests, or thighs, for example, and concluded that this was the ideal human form: "more human than human."[6]

Unlike the cultures surrounding it, the Egyptian empire had organized and clarified every inch of the human figure against a precise grid. Partly, this grid was tied to maintaining the mindset that a god-man, Pharaoh, deserved supremacy over the rest of humanity. Moreover, the empire wanted its images to last forever, sort of like the completed film. In Egypt's case, the images were literally set in stone, so they required consistency and order. In line with empire standards, we have steadily fashioned our own blend of Egyptian and Greek controls. That is, we have mandated an ideal form and then created a grid to insure for it. Not long ago, I came across an article on reconstructive surgery that examined Marilyn Monroe and Audrey Hepburn as candidates. Surgeons had concluded that both could use plenty of work and a diagram was placed over their countenances to indicate what parts needed to be improved upon and how that might be achieved.

Ancient Greeks believed that if one looked good, one *was* good. They believed that if the gods took human form, they would be beautiful, so naturally, the reverse would also be true. One could become godlike (and by extension, like a god, good) by becoming perfectly beautiful. The public awaited the birth of the promised child of TomKat (Tom Cruise and Katie Holmes) and BrAngelina (Brad Pitt and Angelina Jolie) with the anticipation previously reserved for the Messiah. How perfect will this carefully bred offspring of the gods be? In the case of Baby Cruise, perfect enough to require special birthing methods. In the case of Baby Pitt, perfect enough to close the borders of an entire African country. (The couple gave birth in a clinic in Namibia, which would not admit foreign press without the celebrity couple's written permission).

The far off possibilities dangled before us by nearby movie stars are many, and human perfection is only one, but a deliriously attractive one. So much so that, like our movie idols, Cal-types are willing to slice and dice ourselves at the hands of plastic surgeons that act as our trusted priests as we sacrifice our blood and flesh on the operating table. *I Want a Famous Face*, cried the blunt title of a 2004 "reality" show offering reconstructive surgery to its participants. Those who appeared on *The Swan* that year were less specific, but they too were eager to be chiseled to empire standards. "I don't recognize myself!" wept one young woman after her treatment. "And I love it!"

Soon, we will be able to eliminate the middleman of reconstructive surgery and head straight for the original genetic coding to give us the looks we want. This may be why the empire standards have become so airtight. For the most overlooked story of the past quarter century has been the relationship between major corporations that have divested themselves of chemical interests in favor of genetic ones.[7] The Third Reich tried to impose eugenics to create a master race of blonde, blue-eyed perfection and we considered it an outrage. However, it appears that what could not be coerced can be voluntarily chosen if the culture so directs.[8] Hitler may have lost the war, but not that ultimate mission.

Recently, California led the way in the development of therapeutic cloning by passing a landmark initiative (Proposition 71).

This should surprise no one. According to the *AARP Bulletin* "regions who take the lead in high-tech research tend to make millions, even billions."[9] The same article quotes a medical ethicist's caution that the amount of money at stake "makes it crucial to step back and talk about these issues not in terms of special interests but [within] a broader concept of justice."[10] A drawing accompanies the article, depicting a miner panning for genes. If the get-rich-quick gold rush is our operating metaphor, I don't like our ethical chances.

Are You Working?

When artists ask one another, "Are you working?" they don't necessarily mean, "Are you getting paid?" Dorothy Sayers reminds us that work, especially creative work, is instinctual to us as created beings, and though it may be arduous, it is certainly not a curse.[11] However, there is a curse associated with the fall of man: the curse of having to work in order to make a living.[12] Making a living as an artist seems out of the question for many, especially making a living in Hollywood (although the entertainment business and allied trades comprise one of the Southland's largest employers). The sacrifices that are expected by the entertainment industry go well beyond the usual notions of "hard work." The 2005 documentary *Who Needs Sleep?* explores the grueling demands of "Hollywood's dream factory," including "18+ hour workdays, sometimes for weeks on end." Prompted by the death of an assistant cameraman who fell asleep at the wheel on his way home from a shoot in 1997, the film examines "corporate motives behind the exhausting work grind and the sometimes devastating effects of long hours and sleep deprivation on the lives and families of both casts and crew."[13]

The fact is, artists prove their worthiness to exist in the tiny speck of limelight from our local Mt. Olympus by what they are willing to sacrifice, not how hard they are willing to work. If it were simply hard work we respected, we would treat laborers much better. The idea here is that one's job must become one's life. We need to be driven, even obsessed, by our work in order to be trusted. In short, we need to be devoted to it. This is the major difference between servanthood and servitude— one is voluntary and the other coerced—and that important difference manifests itself in the absence of freedom and the presence of fear.

As a performer, when I paid attention to the work, and not to myself, I enjoyed a sense of freedom that was quite rare for women on stage (or in general, for that matter), and it allowed me to make quite daring choices and to fully explore comedic possibilities. I had wonderful partners on whom I relied heavily, and this sense of community was extended, at our best moments, to the larger community of the audience. I am certain it was this freedom that attracted the interest of agents and producers, yet the day I walked into the offices of the president of NBC I was so filled with anxiety that, if I had been playing the part of a peon in Hollywood's grip, I would have been overacting.

The office resembled nothing so much as Darth Vader's death star, a grey cube with grids on the wall containing network ratings. How does anyone create anything here, I wondered. I knew I'd be expected to be charming and funny and inventive, but I was having trouble breathing. I loosened my jacket button without effect. I loosened my skirt waistband and shifted the top of my panty hose as executives entered and began to ask questions. I had no idea what they were asking, but I agreed to everything. Then I backed out of the room like Dorothy leaving the Wizard of Oz. I don't think I bowed, but I can't be sure.

It is this kind of mystique attached to the industry that now makes my job so difficult, years later, as I attempt to train actors to do good work regardless of the stages or sets on which they will find themselves over time. One of my greatest challenges is to convince students that, despite the media's ongoing call to adopt "the secrets of the stars," there is no voodoo attached to acting itself. If actors are well trained, they need not concern themselves with magical appeal or disapproval, "hot nights, off nights," and the rest of the conjured demons. To be sure, audience responses vary and audition choices can be capricious, but the odds of getting work and doing it well do not rely on superstitious devotional practices of hand-wringing prayers, over-grooming, facial contortion, and fake adulation in pursuit of a producer's blessing. They rely on knowledge of the craft, a willingness to prepare well, an interest in the project or story at hand, a mannerly respect for employers and coworkers, and above all, truthfulness, courage, and concentration—the first things to go when an actor is easily spooked.

None of the work to prepare for acting is flashy, and as we know, the awkward, difficult tasks involved in truly good workmanship are hidden in fan magazines. Unfortunately, they are hidden from a public that includes young actors who think they want to act for a living. For my students to concentrate on what they will look like in a particular role before they have bothered to study the script is a lot like a garage band that spends its entire time trying to come up with a catchy name for themselves instead of rehearsing. But to convince students of this is to do battle with the very culture they seek to enter. I am asking them to stop pretending when pretense seems such a hot commodity.

Work versus Works

In fan magazines, the actor is both inflated and reduced to one who will not necessarily create good work, but good worship, and this calls for an audience of fanatics. Such an audience cannot be relied upon to emerge spontaneously. It must be engineered by what John Caughey calls "imaginary social relationships" between fan and celebrity.[14] These relationships result from several means, most of them image-based, but none so great as the close-up that allows us to gaze into an actor's eyes much longer than we can in normal social relationships. When the close-up was introduced, some viewers fainted at the sight, for to an inexperienced audience, the disembodied moving head is terrifying. Despite the impressive gains in special effects over the years, the most powerful special effect ever created still may be the close-up.

Unfortunately, the close-up hides as much as it reveals. It hides the importance of the actor's entire body, not as an object of reverence, but as a tool for storytelling, all kinds of storytelling in all kinds of environments.[15] It hides environment itself. The close-up favors a certain kind of story that focuses on the problems of individuals and encourages the melodrama to which we are historically prone. "Most women's pictures are as boring and as formulaic as men's pictures," observes Frances MacDormand. "In place of a car chase or a battle scene what you get is an extreme close-up of a woman breaking down. I cry too, maybe three times a week, but it's not in close-up. It's a wide shot. It's in the context of a very large and very mean world."[16]

This is how public focus can be drawn away from world events and toward the individual lives of celebrities, in partial answer to the mystifying question, why should J-Lo's latest feud eclipse news of global warming? As the camera replaces the larger world with individuals who, in some respects, *become the world* to us, they begin to represent social policy to us, not merely personal policy. It is one thing to attempt to emulate celebrity looks, but quite another to achieve celebrity charisma. So Cal-types begin to follow the causes of celebrities and make policy decisions based on their good works (that is, worthy causes) rather than their good work (that is, redemptive storytelling).

Singer Jessica Simpson followed in her idol Angelina Jolie's footsteps when she lobbied members of congress on behalf of a children's charity. A source close to the organization confirmed, "This is her Angelina moment."[17] There are other reasons to care about these causes, reasons that must stem from actual, personal knowledge of and concern over the plight of the world. And I think Californians, especially, know this instinctively. I'm very grateful when a celebrity draws attention to a social problem, via their art or their action (though other forms of educating ourselves wouldn't be a bad idea). But, most of us would agree that concern over social problems ought not rely solely on the capricious goodwill of other humans, regardless of the divine status they've been awarded.

The original translation of the word *charisma* is "breathed grace," and those of us hoping to be charismatic might bear that in mind. The word again suggests the strong, diligent relaxation of the sea otter and importantly refers to breath. "Breathe!" I beg my actors. "Don't pant!" It's as though the adrenaline rush is equivalent to the gold rush, as though the actors feel they must prove their worthiness to occupy the stage by showing the audience how hard they're working, rather than doing the work before the audience shows up and is made to share the actors' stress and strain. Like so much else in California, theatrical success is presumed to be accidental, lucky, the result of pure desire and a weird form of sacrifice that relies on securing magical favor, rather than on developing natural gifts. God asks for obedience, not sacrifice. We are to follow valuable instruction, not try to make our best, uneasy guess at what might manipulate the favor of our nearby/far-off gods.

Gene Edward Veith underscores the difference between doing good work as an artistic endeavor and attempting good works as a spiritual endeavor.[18] Christians ought not think that if they are seeking to evangelize through the arts, the results will automatically be blessed. Work that packs any real power is almost always the result of outstanding technique, diligence, and yes, long hours (though not of a slavish nature). Our work finds favor with God when it is indeed work. However, faith, inspiration, and wonder are also involved, as anyone knows who seeks to rely upon God in the creation of good work, as opposed to trying to use divinity, impress divinity, help divinity out, or even take the place of divinity.

The Church of the Gods

Science may manage to help the general population look like their gods, and behavior modification may help us earn the right to godlikeness, but only Scientology will promise to *make* us gods. Again, there's a kind of grid involved. The old fashioned idols such as Marilyn Monroe, James Dean, and Elvis Presley, though obviously a deathless trinity in and of themselves, are simply too hit-and-miss. They couldn't control their fates and it made them terribly nervous. Fortunately, today's celebrities can take hold of their divine futures via Scientology, "the study and handling of the spirit in relationship to itself, others and all of life."[19] It's no small wonder Tom Cruise doesn't seem to feel the need to watch what he says on *Oprah*. He's bulletproof. Scientology has guaranteed as much.

The plethora of Scientology testing centers in downtown Hollywood, Scientology's mass marketing techniques, and its origins in science fiction may make Scientology seem like a pop phenomenon. But, although it claims to contain "new discoveries about life that have never been known before," we are assured that "Scientology is a religion in the deepest and most traditional sense, for it is concerned with no less than the full rehabilitation of man's innate spiritual self—his capabilities, his awareness and his certainty of his own immortality—and his relationship to the divine." The idea that the rich and famous deserve their wealth and fame because they are a higher species with a special relationship with the divine is an old one. And it is certainly true that Scientology rests on historical religious systems, particularly those of world empires.

The most recent version of the belief that we are one with the cosmos (but some more "one" than others) finds many of its most eloquent arguments in science fiction. James A. Herrick traces science fiction's rising preoccupation over the past hundred years with a spiritual universe rather than a physical one, a universe in which we all share a common spirituality that can be manipulated at will. Inevitably, this thought pattern has allowed for "a pantheistic cosmos inhabited by a superior race of beings developing toward perfection through social engineering and primitive eugenics."[20]

Science fiction writer Arthur C. Clarke may be most famous for authoring *2001: A Space Odyssey*, which some critics considered "a profoundly religious film."[21] Herrick observes that according to Clarke's vision, "Whatever the future of religion . . . it would have to accommodate science, especially evolutionary theory, and it would have to allow for the intervention in human development of more highly evolved beings that we might easily mistake for gods."[22] In this vein, it is significant that Scientology founder L. Ron Hubbard was a science fiction writer of the 1940s and '50s who parlayed his stories into a sort of science religion.

As in the case of physical makeovers mentioned earlier in this chapter, the spiritual makeover guaranteed by Scientology involves systematic analysis and measurements. The process begins with "a professional personality test that uses 200 specially designed questions" to determine one's strengths as well as the weaknesses blocking one's "true potentials." Results are "displayed on a graph . . . which rates you against 20 different personality traits." All this is vital because "your personality determines your future."[23] "If you want your life to be richer and fuller, and you just want to be really happy, then there you go. You need Scientology," testifies one satisfied customer, whose biographical information gives way to her media credits.[24]

Even though "scientology exists to provide help—help for all people—at every strata of life," and is dedicated to social improvements such as "providing real answers to declining literacy levels," it ruefully acknowledges that "we must not forget those individuals upon whom society depends the most," our celebrities.

As the Celebrity Centre website reminds us,

> L. Ron Hubbard once said, "The world is carried on the backs of a desperate few." Unfortunately, it is these desperate few who are often the most neglected. It is for this reason that L. Ron Hubbard saw to the formation of a special Church of Scientology that would cater to these individuals—the artists, politicians, leaders of industry, sports figures, and anyone with the power and vision to create a better world. That church is Celebrity Centre International.
>
> Now one might argue that these individuals already have benefits that many will never have. But, ask any one of them— ask yourself—it can become a lonely world.

Subject to the unusual pressures that come with prominence and responsibility, being looked upon under a microscope for good or bad—these are burdens others can't imagine. Not to mention the counter-attack such individuals are subjected to by those less ambitious who would rather fight to maintain a "status quo" than allow another to attempt a change or improvement.[25]

According to Hubbard, "The artist has an enormous role in the enhancement of today's and the creation of tomorrow's reality." In order to aid celebrities in the creation of a better reality, "Scientology gives one the tools one needs to handle any situation in life. In this sense, Scientology helps the able to become more able." In the calculus of such spiritual Darwinism "the more able" are those who evolve spiritually as well as physically. Scientology "brings spiritual enlightenment to man by way of religious practices that advance him to higher states of spiritual ability and understanding."[26]

Dianetics: The Modern Science of Mental Health, the source text for the Church of Scientology, suggests that "the basic command followed by all life, 'SURVIVE!' is subdivided into 8 dynamics (dynamic meaning urge, drive, or impulse)." Allegedly, one of these dynamics is INFINITY, "also commonly called God,"[27] and the integration of this dynamic will "increase survival" of, presumably, the most spiritually fit. Where might a doctrine of grace enter into such a setup? "Scientology does not owe its help. We have done nothing to cause us to propitiate. Had we done so, we would not now be bright enough to do what we are doing."[28] Evidently, grace is only needed by the less bright.

It's a good thing too, because one must *believe* in the gospel of grace, whereas Scientology asks no one "to accept anything as belief or on faith." True, Scripture tells us "without faith it is impossible to please God,"[29] but that was written nearly two thousand years ago, before God evolved to the eighth dynamic of *Dianetics*. Scientology guarantees results. It is religion that leaves nothing to chance and claims as its primary virtues those to which we sacrifice the most: efficiency and speed.

Humanly Speaking

The green glow from Celebrity Centre International, a Scientology institution in Hollywood, shares the same block of sky as the Celtic cross above Hollywood Presbyterian church, former parish of another celebrity, Bono. Bono laughed and nodded with the rest of U2 when, at the Rock and Roll Hall of Fame induction ceremony, Bruce Springsteen accused him (and himself) of possessing a "Messiah complex." It is this very self-effacing quality that makes Bono such an effective change agent. He realizes he is a mere human trying to save the world, and openly acknowledges this. He does not try to escape his humanity; he confesses it, even embraces it, with or without Christendom's blessing.

Bono has been quick to comment on the irony of a leather-jacketed rock star sharing a conference room with leaders of state as he argued reasons to cancel the debts of the world's poorest nations, particularly those in Africa. He and other members of Jubilee 2000 have honored the ancient scriptural mandate to forgive financial debts after a certain time when it becomes clear that they cannot be paid and are creating a cycle of increased poverty. Folks didn't like the idea then any more than we do now. We are not evolving or raising our level of consciousness when it comes to money.

Fortunately, the principles of Scientology "provide the means for an individual to become capable of solving his own problems." Hear that, Africa? "He is then in a position where he not only can sort out his own life, but having learned to better conditions around him, he can also effectively help others."[30] It's not clear how this spiritual trickle down theory works, but one thing seems certain. It takes a hyperevolved personality to pull it off, something akin to Carl Sagan's "super-evolved, god-like alien beings" in *Contact*, "controlling the destiny, not just of the earth, but of the universe itself."[31]

Located on the stunning Big Sur coastline and perched at what seems the edge of the world, the Esalen Institute is a pricey, gorgeous "alternative educational center devoted to the exploration of what [science fiction writer] Aldous Huxley called the 'human potential,' the world of unrealized human capacities that lies beyond the imagination."[32] Esalen offers many classes designed to glean divine knowledge from nature that will facilitate our evolutionary process. It's a tantalizing offer. However, as Herrick notes, "Nature must be explored as a gift that points us to the giver, not as an Aladdin's lamp waiting to yield up to the diligent inquirer unlimited powers both physical and spiritual."[33]

Esalen is possibly the classiest of the spiritual awareness and self-improvement programs in California, but there are hundreds of smaller outfits with the same goals. I noticed one in Monterey that creates "sacred spaces: sanctuaries and habitats that nourish the soul." Once more, the chances to create such spaces seem to expand in direct proportion to one's income. But the overall goal appears to be creating spaces that "elaborate on who we are" so "it's like coming home to one's self."[34]

Speaking as one who could use more than her share of self improvement and spiritual enlightenment, I have to say I have never made much genuine progress by "coming home to myself." My self is sort of a mess, frankly, that is usually improved and enlightened against my will, if at all. Throughout college and grad school, I made the rounds of spiritual pyramid schemes from here to India, and I never achieved anything like the perfect spiritual state they hawked. To the contrary, I began to diminish a bit as a human being. Imagine my surprise when I returned to my native Christianity only to find it had been ransacked by many of the same bankrupt methods.

Scientology could learn a thing or two from the grids and systems the new evangelicalism is marketing, all designed to enhance our character and make us better people, as though the purpose of Christ's suffering was to fine-tune our personalities and make the church as appealing and influential as Hollywood is. But like the plastic surgery mushrooming in our state, plastic movements that borrow the "secrets of the stars" abound, and Christendom is far from immune. Meanwhile, the essential truth Christianity has going for it, namely, oh yeah, Christ, frequently seems, in the words of Barbara Ehrenreich "gagged and tethered to a tent pole" in the church parking lot.[35]

The gospel of grace comes up less and less often, and it's a small wonder. For we are busying ourselves with spiritual evolution, much as the Scientologists are, and in our pursuit of spiritual perfection, a gospel that can only be good news to the imperfect seems awkwardly out of place. "What we see in the garden of Eden is humanity striving to forge its own path to spiritual significance by seeking to be like God," according to Herrick, and our current pseudoscientific methods "perpetuate this most destructive of spiritual fantasies." I'm not too concerned about these methods in Scientology, but when I see them at church, it makes my blood run cold. We have only one really interesting message, "that salvation is built on transforming grace, not on an evolving human race,"[36] and we ourselves must become reacquainted with that message before we can share it with others.

7

Sunshiny Mournings

Funerals

The Cal-type is expected to customize our most profound ceremonies to make them more meaningful. Sometimes it's easy to forget that they are meaningful enough in and of themselves, and may not need our help. Last summer, I drove some distance to the memorial service of my former manager and good friend. I was shaken to the core by his passing and truly needed the opportunity to grieve with friends and family. No such chance. This was not really a funeral, or a recognizable memorial service, for that matter. This was what we have come to know in California as the celebration of a life. My manager had represented a good many comedians and rock bands. He had rescued several of us from oblivion and ushered us into relative success. I was grateful to him and felt there was plenty to remember about him with others.

But because he was quite a funny guy, and the assembly was filled with stand-up comics, the remarks became performances and the entire event nonstop entertainment, with bands playing and occasional dancing. A well-loved local celebrity acted as emcee and kept things rolling, even on the rare occasion when a speaker became tearful. This was certainly not California's first, well, funeral party. We conduct these events with some regularity within the entertainment community. Often, such gatherings turn into networking and promotional opportunities as well. I hope I never again feel pressured to make people laugh at a memorial service, but I might. California-ism just doesn't offer many other options for how to grieve.

A visiting scholar from Kenya once asked me to explain our attitude toward death. He said that in his country, when someone died and the family was unable to retrieve the body and hold on to it in the grieving process, they had to go to the witch doctor to be healed. He said he noticed that here, the bodies were "snatched away" from families by emergency vehicles or undertakers, and that people were not given sufficient opportunity to grasp loved ones and wail over them with others in the community. The next time most of us see the bodies of our deceased, if at all, they are wearing makeup and are usually dressed in something nice. Those attending the funeral rarely weep loudly, and if anything, they seem unusually quiet and still.

He wondered how we escaped illness as a result; why no need for the witch doctor? I told him I didn't think we did escape illness, but that we call our witch doctors psychiatrists. I added that most of our grieving was an individual rather than communal act, something we typically did on our own or in the company of a professional. After that conversation, the questions raced through my head: Do we perform certain mourning rituals here as people elsewhere? Or do we merely *perform*? Public wailing may seem theatrical to us, but perhaps we calm and collected mourners are actually the trained actors.

The traditional purpose for wearing black during mourning periods is and was so that if a person broke down in the marketplace or elsewhere, those around them would understand and allow them to grieve, perhaps even joining them. Yet in our society of strangers, if we begin to weep at the supermarket, we likely head for the car before we can be seen. We are ashamed of our tears and must cry privately, fix our faces, and pull ourselves together before appearing in public, even if the public is a small group of friends or family.

My father-in-law was a part-time clown. When he died and was cremated, the clowns who worked with him at the local union showed up at his memorial service in full makeup to pay tribute to him. Later, my niece explained to a friend who'd never attended a funeral that most funerals didn't include clowns. And though this may be true, most of them here do include heavy makeup.

Show Time

The Loved One, Evelyn Waugh's scorching indictment of California culture, sets its story in a mock version of famed Forest Lawn cemetery called Whispering Glades. The customs of the ornately themed funeral/amusement park, referred to by its creator as "The Dream," are likened repeatedly to those of the nearby entertainment industry, with its reliance on cosmetics, costuming, and hype. An enthusiastic promoter describes a hideously deformed corpse fixed "so it looked like it was his wedding day"[1] and another corpse is "dressed as though for an evening party."[2] An idea for a popular burial garment is said to have come from quick-change artists, "enabling one to dress the loved one without disturbing the pose."[3]

The point may easily be taken from the novel, written in 1948, that not only are Cal-types expected to perform for one another at funerals, but the dearly departed are expected to perform for us as well, their identities formed and reformed in death as in life, to create more pleasing effects. In this enterprise, the actual loved one is anything but. And whatever else we might conclude about the deceased, the most essential conclusion seems to be that they wouldn't want us to grieve; they'd want us to be happy. Isn't that the goal of the entire universe: to make us happy?

Although "morticians, however eminent, are not paid like film stars,"[4] Waugh writes, there is a high price tag for memorial special effects. Much of the cost results from the "very individual" chosen accommodations,[5] such as a memorial cite made to resemble a historical Oxford church; "more than a replica, it is a reconstruction . . . a symbol of the soul of the loved one who starts from here on the greatest success story of all time."[6] Needless to say, on these unholy grounds where the protagonist feels himself "in the Egypt of the Pharaohs,"[7] there is little in the way of sound theology. Waugh laments: "Liturgy in Hollywood is the concern of the stage rather than of the clergy."[8]

"I expect to be head chaplain at Whispering Glades," observes Waugh's protagonist. "Something in the metaphysical seventeenth-century manner, appealing to the intellect rather than to crude emotion . . . verbose, ingenious and doctrinally quite free of prejudice. I have been thinking a good deal about my costume, full sleeves, I think."[9] His proclamation follows this earlier conversation with a professional "Reverend."

"Tell me, how does one become a nonsectarian clergyman?"

"One has the Call."

"Yes, of course; but after the Call, what is the process? I mean is there a non-sectarian bishop who ordains you?"

"Certainly not. Anyone who has received the Call has no need for human intervention."

"You just say one day 'I am a non-sectarian clergyman' and set up shop?"

"There is considerable outlay. You need buildings. But the banks are usually ready to help. Then of course, what one aims at is a radio congregation."

"A friend of mine has the Call."

"Well, I should advise him to think twice about answering it. The competition gets hotter every year, especially in Los Angeles."[10]

It would be easy to laugh all this off as great satire, were the real goings on at celebrity cemeteries less outlandish. Walter Brueggemann writes, "When we suffer from amnesia, every form of serious authority for faith is in question, and we live unauthorized lives of faith and practice unauthorized ministries."[11] In the absence of any historical liturgical practice, Cal-types tend to create our own kinds of "liturgies," generally overproduced performance pieces that unintentionally divert attention from the eternal and communal in order that the deceased may be remembered for their temporal, individual, outstanding lives.

Forever Enterprises

Billing itself as the "Resting Place of Hollywood's Immortals," the Hollywood Forever Cemetery (owned by Forever Enterprises) is unique, according to its website, "not only because of the famous people interred there" such as Rudolph Valentino, Jane Mansfield, and Tyrone Power, but because it offers "special services available at no other cemetery in the world. For example [its] Funeral chapel is equipped for live worldwide webcasts of funeral services and LifeStory tributes. Housed in the Library of Lives, LifeStories are composed of film clips, photos, audio tapes, and writings gathered with the help of professional LifeStory specialists" to create an interactive tribute to the departed.[12]

This is the subject of the 2004 science fiction film *Final Cut*. Set in a world with memory implants, Robin Williams plays a cutter, someone with the power of final edit over people's recorded histories. The film's tagline is: "Every moment of your life recorded. Would you live it differently?" Clearly, however, with the editing powers at our disposal, the message we may be taking is that there is little need to live life well. Our lives will all be fictionalized anyway, thanks in large part to our technologies. John Cloud observes that the Hollywood Forever Cemetery creates "a way for people not to dodge mortality but to shape it to their liking," as it makes possible "a kind of manufactured immortality, a heavily edited performance of someone's life that shunts aside what was [once] a cemetery's focus: the end."[13]

Television, according to Bill McKibben, makes powerful contributions to our attitude toward "the end." Given the relentless continuity of programming, television never ends. More to the point, the subject of death is given surprisingly little serious concern in that programming. "Almost no one talks about death on television," nor the actual results of death, "which is odd, considering the number of corpses."[14] Nothing seems to be permanently affected by the carnage pictured on the screen.

Contrasting the solemn, decorous funeral of President Warren Harding in 1923 with the 2004 funeral of Ronald Reagan, "supersized to satisfy our bottomless appetite for the mediathon, an epic form of TV news," Frank Rich believes that "the Reagan outpouring, much of it carried out by bubbly TV-camera-seeking citizens in halter tops and shorts, was grief lite" by comparison. Rich notes that amid the "incessant hyperbole [that] becomes as numbing as Muzak . . . national mourning was giving way to national boredom," adding "Harding's huge turnout didn't alter his hapless historical fate, but at least it was a genuine event."[15]

Time will tell whether or not Reagan's presidency has a historical fate of any kind, for "as the Los Angeles Times reported, 90 percent of the 55 million pages of his papers is still off-limits to scholars at the presidential library where he was entombed."[16] Rich further reminds us that "a 2001 George W. Bush executive order could restrict access to every modern president's historical record indefinitely."[17] This matters a great deal. The historical amnesia we are enabling on the national level is a reflection of the personal amnesia we are experiencing on the immediate level. Furthermore, both may be the result of a psychic battering we are taking from commercial interests that routinely trade in human loss without so much as blinking.

Everyone Back to Work

"Grieving is a luxury we could not afford," states a character in Stephen Spielberg's miniseries, *Into the West*. When loved ones were lost along the westward trail to California, survivors had to keep moving or be lost. And this is the philosophy to which we still seem to cling, even though we crawled off our wagons some time ago. After all, there's still a high price to be paid to live in California, and the bills won't pay themselves, you know. The average work leave for bereavement is three to five days.

What we don't notice is this: when societies are robbed of their capacity for grief, it is bad for people but good for business. We are expected to show our courage, our character, our spirit that built the West, by our tough refusal to weep, much less to solicit comfort. "Empires live by numbness," writes Brueggemann.[18]

Not long ago, a woman in my exercise class lost her young son suddenly in a work accident. When the class instructor informed us of the tragedy by way of announcing a hasty fundraiser, she was quick to add that the grieving woman would *never* have asked for help on her own. We were doing this on our own initiative, "just to, you know, help, kind of." The young instructor was also quick to apologize for any "negative energy" she was creating by her announcement. "Sorry," she grimaced. "We like to keep the air positive here."

She was remarkably nervous that our routine—our puny, unimportant workout—was being momentarily diminished, and I was ashamed. Exactly how shallow and mean-spirited must a people have become in order to intimidate one another thus? Are we not the perfect patsies of an empire that thrives on the assumption that the really important thing, regardless of our circumstances, is for everyone to get back to work as quickly and efficiently as possible, and "keep the air positive" as we do so? A student told me about a buddy of his from church who had just lost his mother. When asked how he was doing in the grieving process, he replied "Great! I did that last week." I'm guessing this is taking the concept of time management a step too far.

Getting Over It

An Australian neighbor of mine once told me that his dog of many years had died and it had undone him. "I'll never get over it," he said. "Wouldn't want to, really." This declaration was a revelation to me, but of course it should not have been. Why would anyone want to remain unchanged by major loss? Isn't at least one point of loving that we are not the same for having loved?

Contrast this with an incident in my classroom this year. A student I know well ran from her desk so suddenly that I followed her down the hall and into the restroom, where I found her sitting on the floor in a corner, rocking back and forth and weeping. When I asked her the problem, she confessed her sister had died during the spring season. "This time of year is always hard on me," she sobbed. "Why of course," I nodded, to which she suddenly cried, "But it's been eight years! I should be over it by now!" The implications startled me. This very young woman had been struggling alone since she was a very young girl, feeling, among other things, guilty about mourning. Moreover, she had been a student of mine for four years and this was my first knowledge of any trauma. She was always smiling, after all.

It is as though a stun gun has been leveled against this most basic and ancient human rite of (and right to) mourning. Brueggemann suggests this is precisely the case within the mentality of an empire that cannot afford a hint of unhappiness. Within this cultural framework, any problem we experience that cannot be solved by the right products or services must be an imaginary problem. Existential pain and metaphysical responses (unless there is a buck to be made from them) are really too complicated, murky, and uncomfortable, not to mention time consuming, to warrant much consideration.

And so the Cal-type is denied any large hope that there is more to life and death than meets the eye, as our imaginations are commandeered by a series of tidy little hopes instead. I am expected to hope that if I jog long enough, or purchase the right vitamins, or hold out for the right stem cell research, or reduce stress in my life (including the stress of grief), I might postpone the personal death issue indefinitely. Everything is all right so long as I say it's all right. However, "real criticism begins in the capacity to grieve because that is the most visceral announcement that things are not right—either in the dean's office or in our marriage or in the hospital room. And as long as the empire can keep the pretense alive that things are all right, there will be no real grieving and no serious criticism."[19] Most important, there will be no growth, no personal revolution, no hope.

As an alternative to the empire mentality illustrated by the ancient kingdoms of Egypt, for example, Brueggemann describes a community of hope such as was mobilized by Moses, one energized by prophetic imagination. Prophetic imagination is generated by a shared and sustained *cry* to God that breaks through the imposed numbness of the daily grind (including the literal grinding of straw to clay to build the immortalizing pyramids of the pharaohs who pictured their reigns as more or less permanent). The cry comes from those desperate for an alternative that seems beyond possibility. It is a cry of grief followed by a cry for help.

People who have lost their little hopes can and must beg for a big hope. But in order for the lament to occur, folks must have some memory of what has happened and is happening to them and to others. In other words, our only hope for changing injustices is to snap out of our trances long enough to grieve. Mourning may constitute the ultimate revolution in a happy-go-lucky, business-as-usual empire. Christ asked us to continue the practice we call Holy Communion in remembrance of him. The assumption is that we are *capable* of remembrance, that we have not gotten over Christ's life, have not gotten over his crucifixion, and have not gotten over his resurrection. It's all supposed to be a very big deal and when it stops being a big deal, we're in terrible spiritual trouble.

Ironically, the numb behavior required by the empire, which may be intended by us as a form of stoicism, is often counter-courageous. Actual courage requires the willingness to endure suffering, not to deny it. At a Harvard commencement address, Alexander Solzhenitsyn observed that the most striking feature of the American character is a decline in courage.[20] Oddly enough, we can only become courageous by *doing something brave*, in this case, actually risking painful experiences. And as long as our culture insists we keep a stiff upper lip, we may remain cowardly, as startling as that may seem. Indeed, nothing at all may change within us, which is precisely the intention of a culture that relies upon and profits from predictable behavior in every area of life.

Thus we have come to participate in what psychologists call "predictable risk," which seems an oxymoron if I ever heard one. These are death defying, or what we might more rightly call death denying, antics intended to demonstrate our courage. A fine example of this controlled fear factor can be found in the Tower of Terror at Disney's California Adventure. In this fabrication of a haunted Hollywood hotel (is there any other kind of Hollywood hotel?), an "elevator" we share with other terror-seekers suddenly gives way to a free falling ride of genuine physical shock.

I can honestly state that my only reason for experiencing this ride was to prove I still have what it takes, whatever that means. And by way of solid evidence, photographs are taken automatically during the scariest parts of the ride to chronicle our fright. We're real survivors, all right, and I can purchase the T-shirt at the Tower of Terror's own private boutique to prove it. I am very brave so long as I am not required to do anything genuinely painful.

In Colton, California, the cemetery where my relatives are buried is populated by more than its share of teenagers, most of whom did not die of natural causes. I walk the grounds silently contemplating the possible facts of their lives. How many were taking a "controlled risk," such as breaking speed laws, experimenting with drugs, hanging out with a gang, or taking some other risk over which they ended up losing control? Could the price of genuine courage attached to more noble causes be any more costly?

Memory Making

It is worth noticing that many post-modern films (*Memento*, *Fight Club*, *Eternal Sunshine of the Spotless Mind*, and so on) interrelate themes of amnesia and numbness with the recovery of pain and hope through memory. All these films deal with the fragility and malleability of memory, as the characters conduct a frustrating and occasionally fruitless search for the past and its vital effect on their present. I am struck by the impact of these films on my students, who seem to find in them a critical voice for the major issues and grievances of their generation.

One such film is *Garden State*, which concerns the journey of Zach, a small-time actor living in Hollywood who must return to New Jersey for his mother's funeral. In the opening scene, eminent destruction threatens his crashing plane, co-passengers shriek with terror as he sits placidly acknowledging nothing. In the next scene, we understand why, for he faces a medicine cabinet with a sea of prescription drugs. Soon we will learn that his mother's death follows her tortured history of depression and physical paralysis owing to an accident Zach indirectly caused. He has been medicated ever since, under orders from his psychiatrist father.

At the funeral, Zach tolerates a terrible rendition of "Three Times a Lady," sung by a neighbor who, it turns out, has sewn him a shirt made from the same "gorgeous" fabric Zach's dead mother used to redesign the bathroom. There ensues a series of awkward, monosyllabic conversations with friends, an endless drug party, and a dismal morning after. Following these hopelessly inadequate mourning rituals, Zach meets a pathological liar who shows genuine grief and vulnerability at a homespun funeral for her dead hamster (whose accident *she* has indirectly caused). When Zach attempts to make jokes about the situation, she scolds him. "That's not funny," she says, before apologizing to the hamster and concluding, "you were a good pet. I hope you liked me." From this point, Zach embarks upon a series of traumatic events that will lead him, eventually, to a healthy embrace of actual experience in favor of the drug-induced amnesia he has known. His memory is jogged. While sitting fully clothed in an empty bathtub with his new friend, Zach remembers a small but genuine moment with his mother, and a single tear falls from his eye, a souvenir that is caught in a paper cup. "I should put it in a scrapbook," says Zach. "If I had a scrapbook."

He has determined to mourn what he can mourn, and to risk whatever feelings are the cost of loving fragile humans, which is probably the bravest and dearest thing any of us does, ever. He takes himself off drugs and faces his father with the question, "Why do we have to be happy all the time? What's wrong with just being alive?" One is reminded of Edith Wharton's observation in her short story *Xingu* that "if only we'd stop trying to be happy we could have a pretty good time." Zach understands the way back to hope is through experience and not away from it. As Brueggemann put it, "Only anguish leads to life, only grieving leads to joy and only embraced endings permit new beginnings."[21] Jesus wept at his friend's funeral because he "knew what we numb ones must always learn again: a) that weeping must be real because endings are real; and b) that weeping permits newness."[22]

Daring to Hope

Without our histories, there can be no future, and without our futures, there can be no hope. We must retain our memories, however painful, and our neighbors must help us do so. Instead of warmed over pop ballads performed at graveside or the inarticulate grunting meant to substitute for legitimate condolences, Zach's Jewish neighbors in *Garden State* might have called upon the truly useful Jewish ceremony of sitting shiva. The tradition requires mourners to sit and recall all the memories possible about the deceased, and disallows them to leave the house or do any work to take their minds off the pain. Meanwhile, neighbors come to remind mourners of every good and loving act of the departed—the purpose of which is to intensify the mourner's grief. It is believed that the only way to true renewal is through the frank acknowledgement of what is irrecoverably lost from the past.

Ultimately, when we love people we make ourselves vulnerable to terribly ephemeral creatures, and whether we like it or not, the only surefire way to avoid this vulnerability is probably to love people less. *Batman Begins*, directed by *Memento* filmmaker Christopher Nolan, contains a chilling speech on the subject. "You begin to wish the person you loved had never been born, so that you wouldn't feel the pain of losing them." Tempting as the escape from grief may be, it's really a very dangerous business and cannot be done without escaping people altogether. Instead of escaping, what we need to do is stick around and attempt to make things better. But when we are not allowed to acknowledge our own grief, how on earth will we be able to acknowledge the grief of our neighbors, much less our distant, invisible neighbors who may be suffering at our hands without our awareness?

Not surprisingly, the *Batman Begins* character making the above speech is seeking revenge, which is one possible response when we are not allowed to grieve properly. Many take revenge against themselves via cutting rituals or other dysfunctional practices. However, there are countless forms of revenge we take against others, both personally and publicly. Ultimately, we may support national and international retaliations, even misguided ones, when we have no other way to work through pain and fear.

After the World Trade Center tragedy of September 11, 2001, we were drowned in the feverish production of American flag artifacts and hoped that the vitality of our dear symbol would survive its placement on bikinis and troll dolls. It was vaguely disheartening to some that, rather than being encouraged to reinvigorate our citizenship by familiarizing ourselves with the US constitution, for example, we were to demonstrate our patriotism by continuing to buy things. How could we hope to negotiate the pressing issues that were sure to arise from so great an attack, some of us wondered, when the town hall had been replaced by the shopping mall?

In all, the effects upon us have lingered at the surface ever since, a shift in content rather than pattern, which remains pretty firmly rooted in melodramatic constructs. These have ranged from the "two-sided" presentation of news stories that in fact have more than two sides, to country music videos offering terrorists ultimatums, to the everlasting parade of action films and comedies featuring bad guys pitted against good guys with the same character defects.

America seems at once comforted and dissatisfied with this steady diet. We are kept preoccupied yet remain disquieted. We intuit that we are dealing with realities that cannot be squeezed into our usual modes of storytelling. Perhaps this instinct is behind the renewed interest in fantasy. We seem to require a template beyond the everyday in which to picture ourselves coping. G. K. Chesterton tells us that fairy tales endure because they offer us a way to imagine average people behaving with courage, kindness, ingenuity, and nobility in an exotic, strange, and often-dangerous environment.[23]

On the other hand, less wholesome blockbusters invite us to move in the opposite direction. We are given movie stars and other newsmakers who are weirder, smarter, richer, more beautiful, or just plain more important than we are, handling our altered environment as though it belonged in the same old plot and making our challenges seem sort of boring. No one really learns much in such stories. No particular moral reasoning, or reasoning of any kind, is encouraged or expected of the audience. Biases are reinforced as we are temporarily warehoused in inactivity, having spent another evening *not* getting to know our neighbors, families, or Bibles; and our entertainment increasingly leaves us as it found us, if not the worse for wear.

Mainstream popular culture for the most part is too preoccupied sustaining itself to worry about sustaining the public. It is innately less capable of redeeming or enlightening tragic events than of clouding or beguiling our genuine concerns and keeping us from thinking too long or too hard about anything. In some respects, the popular culture industry is both inmate and warden of its own narrow prison yard. It must toe the line of its own creation, having made that line of products irrevocably "popular" with the American public, therefore reliably marketable, and therefore the only line financial backers will likely produce. It is true that many stories told through screen and song attempt to create reflective thought in audiences. But for the most part, commercial culture offers only what it can, and that simply is not enough, on its own, to educate, nourish, and encourage us, nor to provoke the kind of thought, dialogue, and apprehension of truth and meaning needed in such uncertain times.

Public Mourning

There have been over sixty-five hundred proposals submitted for a public memorial to the World Trade Center tragedy. These competitive entries from professional companies must conform to forty standards, and big money is involved. Alternatively, and importantly, on Santa Monica Beach in California, every week since February 15, 2004, a grassroots public memorial dubbed "Arlington West" [24] is erected by the local chapter of Veterans for Peace and other volunteers to honor soldiers fallen in the Iraq War. Visitors read the names, ages, rank, hometown, and circumstance of death, write the name of a fallen military person on a piece of paper along with any thoughts or sentiments, and attach this to a cross along with a flower. These are the kinds of efforts, both individual and corporate, cropping up throughout California, as intentional refusals to pretend that death doesn't matter. In a different way, innovations here such as home funerals or green burials follow a similar principle. Death needs to be acknowledged for what it is, here and now.

Arlington West provides such striking counterpoint to the glitz and glamour of the imperial Hollywood Forever that it is hard to believe they lie within scant miles of one another. The fact is, Californians really are willing to trade the beauty and escape offered by our vistas for enduring and meaningful purposes. So at the beach where surfers and bunnies usually frolic, a blanket of crosses covers the sand. Arlington West offers a place to mourn, reflect, contemplate, grieve, honor, and acknowledge those who've lost their lives, and to reflect upon the true cost of war. We can continue in this direction.

Hamlet is the story of a college student who is not allowed to grieve the death of his father, a tragedy followed much too quickly by the marriage celebration of his mother and his uncle, the new king. The royal consciousness is eager to get back to normal. But Hamlet spends better than three hours of stage time discussing all the reasons why things will never be normal again, and why things are definitely not okay. Interestingly, he is prohibited from taking revenge on his father's murderer as long as he is grieving, which begs the question, can one retaliate and grieve at the same time, or is retaliation an understandable escape from grief?

At the end of the day, Hamlet must be willing to face his own death, as discussed in the "to be or not to be" speech, in order to take civil action of any kind, and so must we. Of course we don't want to be reminded of our deaths. God especially is troubled by death, and so should we be, in my opinion. We cannot feel true compassion for others until we acknowledge that we are all in the same boat. There's a reason churches once came with graveyards. We are all going to die, and it's nothing about which to be cavalier.

The ninth chapter of the Book of St. Matthew reminds us that Christ felt compassion, which might properly be translated "churning in his guts," when he saw that the people in all the towns and villages were harassed and helpless, also translated "noisy, angry, confused, *flayed, and prostrate.*" The implication in this passage is that powerful others are doing the harassing[25] and someone must intercede on behalf of the oppressed.

Brueggemann writes, "Quite clearly, the one thing the dominant culture cannot tolerate or co-opt is compassion, the ability to stand in solidarity with the victims of the present order. It can manage charity and good intentions, but it has no way to resist solidarity with pain or grief. So the structures of competence and competition stand helpless before the one who groaned the groans of those who are hurting. And in their groans they announce the end of the dominant social world."[26]

Hamlet makes a mess out of things because he acts alone in his wild-eyed grief, confusion, and revenge. The terrible final scene appears to be Shakespeare's judgment against such a hopeless societal predicament, leaving the question echoing throughout the last centuries: why didn't anyone help this poor guy? I know this much. If we had any inkling of the possible losses and private agonies of the stranger standing next to us at the bank, or driving next to us on the highway, or phoning us for telemarketing companies, I'll bet, even if we cannot "groan the groans of those who are hurting," at least we'd be a tiny bit more kind.

8

'Til Death Do Us Part, or Whatever

Marriage

Though we may be known for our colorful funerals in California, we are willing to don more stark and stylish colors at our weddings. My superstitious Irish grandmother would have thrown sticks at a bridesmaid wearing black, unconvinced that it made fashion sense; but she knew nothing of bridal magazines. Our marriage rituals may not have much in the way of tradition behind them, but at times they have seemed as solidly entrenched and as readily identifiable as any ancient rite. They've had to be. Annually, weddings represent a seven billion dollar industry in California, far and away the highest in the union, with the average cost of a Californian wedding hovering around thirty-two thousand dollars.[1] As in other areas of life, the folk rituals that once defined normative behavior at weddings have often given way to the customs of Hollywood, customs that "simultaneously exalt and trivialize the hallowed institution of marriage."[2]

Recently, I've attended more and more ceremonies that, without skirting such customs altogether, have insured that the wedding retained ritual elements that were liturgical, thoughtful, meaningful, poetic, sometimes ancient, and altogether moving. They were beautiful weddings, certainly, but they were quite a bit more than that. Such weddings remind all those gathered of the most profound and lasting truths concerning marriage, family, and faith; they enrich and ennoble us all. And, maybe due to their expressive creativity, color, and conviviality, I see these weddings as uniquely Californian. I am excited to see this resistance to the McWedding of California-ism, and the values/beliefs such weddings seem to promote. There's a lot to resist.

Some years ago, I attended a Southern California wedding that so rigidly conformed to pop cultural conventions as to codify a kind of standard. It took place in an enormous church that was really opulent, for an art-free environment, with indirect "glamour lighting" such as that used by film studios. Before the ceremony came a video slide show of what seemed to be every photograph ever taken of the bride and groom. The presentation was set to music and lasted through four power ballads. Midway, my husband wondered whether there would be an intermission. Eventually a live singer delivered another pop ballad with carefully manufactured emotion, and the stick-thin bridal party outfitted from the pages of *Modern Bride* took their positions in beauty pageant formation across the altar/stage. After an entertaining homily from the pastor and the repetition of vows, the couple was pronounced man and wife and the newlyweds danced down the aisle to the music of Frank Sinatra.

Afterward, we chatted too long with friends in the parking lot before proceeding to the reception and got horribly lost on the way. Frantic and embarrassed, we stumbled into the reception approximately an hour and a half after the wedding, but the bridal party was still posing for photographs. We took our seats and waited for the emcee to announce their arrival amid general applause. Then we continued to sit as we watched the bride and groom dance and exchange meaningful gazes, flanked by their gorgeous attendants. Above the dance floor was a video feed of their larger than life faces. "Gee. It's almost like being here," joked my husband.

We are exceedingly fond of this couple, as we are of so many couples that have enacted many of the same marriage rituals. The slender involvement we had that day with the bride and groom reveals an important dynamic of the Cal-type wedding. Sometimes, there has been less pressure for the couple to be hospitable than to perform for their guests and to make themselves at least as beautiful and beguiling as the average soap opera couple. This is not to say that vows and greetings aren't important, just that they've been made part of a larger script that includes many production elements. The wedding as mediated event can rival the wedding as historical event.

There's some apprehension that guests will be bored or otherwise made to feel uncomfortable by the ceremonies themselves, particularly religious ceremonies. I've heard people worrying about a ceremony going too long in the same way pastors worry about over-an-hour church services. Guests are intended to be entertained as well as engaged. As a matter of fact, some Californians have on occasion charged admission to their weddings, in a manner of speaking. Since the wedding cost per guest is so high, instead of purchasing a gift from the usual registry, one might be asked to contribute to the bride's pedicure, for example, or some other component of the wedding production aesthetic. It's not really fair for the wedding couple to shoulder the expense of this glossy spectacle when presumably all will enjoy it.

The wedding party, which California-ism might make the stars of the event, typically has been introduced at the reception in an amplified fanfare once reserved for the Oscar runway. It is hard to know whether the wedding party wants this kind of ballyhoo or if the deejay acts on his own initiative to make his job seem more essential. An important dynamic of the wedding spectacular seems to lie in the growing population of broadcasting majors who need work. Many aspiring disc jockeys, derailed by the increased automation of radio programming, do wedding gigs to keep their skills up. Rather than adjusting their performance patter to fit the occasion, often deejays have tended to adjust the occasion to fit the patter.

We attended a wedding on the seashore that was uncommonly organic, sweet, and moving. Yet at the reception, the deejay kept a generically funky techno beat blaring as he frantically worked the room, asking elderly guests, "Hey, where ya' from? Are you ready for a little Fitty Cent? Maybe a little Tupac?" (This was meant as a gag, but I have known traditionally dressed Korean grandmothers of the groom who were forced to dance to songs by both of these rappers.) The deejay continued thus throughout the night ready to fill the first trace of silence. "Yes, ladies and gentlemen, Southern California is the place to be tonight, with the new Mr. and Mrs. . . . ."

"Here's a little thing we like to call the father of the bride dance," he cried, and well into the "money dance," he informed us there was "no line to dance with the groom." During toasts from the best man and maid of honor, the deejay faded in film soundtracks so we would know how to feel about what was being said. Once, he accidentally played the theme from *Jaws* but made up for it by demanding four rounds of applause for the toasts. Then, "Don't go away, ladies and gentlemen, coming up soon . . . cake!" The only moment words failed him was the one when they might have done him some good. The power went out and all the technologies failed, including the lights. Everything was utterly still, and in the semi-darkness we saw the deejay staring down at his microphone and vast soundboard with the countenance of a six-year-old whose ice cream has fallen off the cone. He seemed unable to communicate without the media that surrounded him.

Covenants and Contracts

Nothing is more understandable to me than entertaining guests. One of the most enjoyable receptions I've ever attended featured an improvised talent show of wedding guests who entertained for and with the bride and groom all evening. Show business friends performed at my reception, and my own band played at my daughter's. These occasions seemed to call for big parties, and I'm the first to confess that conversations with old friends took a backseat to making sure everyone was dancing. What interests me is the way that our natural instinct to celebrate and/or personalize weddings has been rerouted into the binding conventions of consumer culture. I saw the writing on the wall when a little girl from church approached me at my wedding and as I smiled hello, demanded with makeshift autograph pad in hand, "Are there some more famous people here?"

Yet opulent images, hype, and identification with celebrities are probably the least menacing of our inherited marketing practices. More sobering is the subtle redefinition of vital wedding terms such as "promise" to mean "potential" rather than "covenant." Within California-ism, making promises, taking vows, just doesn't seem to have much pizzazz. But concentrating on the promising possibilities of the newlyweds and their dazzling future, well that's kind of fascinating. The prenuptial contract illustrates the Cal-type's attitudes toward the marriage promise. One such contract "guarantees Danielle Spencer a minimum $15 million payout if she stays with Russell Crowe for at least three years," according to *Women's Wear Daily*.[3] Our promises are conditional, being based on marriage contract and not marriage covenant. We're making a deal. I'm afraid it's something else we picked up from ogling the marriages of movie stars, models, and moguls.

The mind-set encouraged is this: if both partners keep up their end of the bargain and live up to their potential, well then, keep buying. But if one of them begins to put on weight or show their age or some other human frailty, the deal could be off. And applying the precepts of California-ism, the abandoned partner really would have no one to blame but him or herself. After all, letting oneself go reveals a deficiency of character and not only that, but with plastic surgery so readily available, how could one go without it and risk offending the

general public as well as one's spouse? Why should people be
any less consumable commodities than anything else designed
to make us happy?

Romance "has been permeated by the logic of exchange,"
writes sociologist Phillip Vannini,[4] who later notes, "Two interconnected processes are at work: the romanticization of commodities and the commodification of romance. As production
and consumption have expanded, mass communication has
been transmitting to the public a visual idea of love as spectacle."[5] In his discussion of marriage proposal rituals, Vannini
maintains that social actors "attempt to be believable and acceptable by staging ideal versions of their fronts" (that is, their
represented selves, settings, and behaviors) "consistent with the
norms, mores and laws of society."[6]

Ironically but predictably, what seems to make us most believable and acceptable is our likeness to the worlds of cinema and
broadcasting. Describing one specific proposal made via video
production, Vannini observes that romance

> must follow the logic of both spectacle and consumption because
> the ethos of interpersonal relationships has been increasingly
> intermixed with the ethic of consumer culture. Aware that a
> specific setting must be in place, the aforementioned performer
> becomes an entertainer, a representation of himself, and pro-
> poses to his girlfriend while playing the role of a Hollywood
> actor and that of a singer. The front becomes credible and real
> when the setting is "magic," the appearance and manner illusory,
> and the drama movie-like.[7]

Waugh's *The Loved One* notes the lack of depth needed to
attach our romances to any poetic, larger-than-life instinct.

> The English poets were proving uncertain guides in the laby-
> rinth of Californian courtship—nearly all were too casual, too
> despondent, too ceremonious, or too exacting; they scolded,
> they pleaded, they extolled. Dennis required salesmanship; he
> sought to present Aimee with an irresistible picture not so much
> of her own merits or even of his, as of the enormous gratifica-

tion he was offering. The films did it; the crooners did it; but not, it seemed, the English poets.[8]

Of the woman Dennis is wooing the author writes,

> She presented herself to the world dressed and scented in obedi-ence to the advertisements. As she grew up the only language she knew expressed fewer and fewer of her ripening needs; the facts which littered her memory grew less substantial; the figure she saw in the looking-glass seemed less recognizably herself. Her heart was broken perhaps, but it was a small inexpensive organ of local manufacture.[9]

A friend of mine used to joke that he dated a girl from New-port Beach and was amazed at the depth of her superficiality. But in such an environment, what is the exact point in working to cultivate one's mind and heart? These things are invisible and cannot be marketed. Thus strong minds and hearts seem inessential to a relationship.

The only area of television in which women share more or less equal representation is in commercials. This is no accident and is especially important in light of the ritualistic power of advertis-ing. Advertisers are hypersensitive to the smallest change in the pulse of American women's lives, since they are reliant upon women to support, among many other markets, a $33-billion-a-year diet industry and a $20-billion-a-year cosmetics industry.[10] Since the early 1950s, when advertising revenues soared to initi-ate a surge in consumer buying habits, women have been heav-ily targeted.[11] Using marketers' reports, Betty Friedan showed that working women were considered too critical to represent a healthy market, but that American housewives' lack of identity and purpose could be manipulated into vast revenues.[12]

At one time, domestic ads were designed to create guilt over hidden dirt and invisible germs and to infuse a false sense of achievement and specialized skill to compensate for the end-less and unrewarding aspects of housework. Advertisers were encouraged to identify household products with quasi-religious feelings, beliefs, and rewards, to fashion a kind of cult around "life-changing" household products and appliances. As more women began to work outside the home, advertisers steadily readjusted their focus so that the manic sale of beauty and diet products eclipsed that of household products. But both markets, to a large extent, depend upon and help sustain the plight of women[13] and the identification of commodities with the quasi-religious.

For beauty and diet products to have the *most* appeal, women need to believe they themselves are somehow incomplete, inadequate, or uninteresting; thus the ad industry has worked overtime to convey that belief.[14] Further, the sale of beauty and diet products relies upon a mythical belief in a perfect woman and in the existence of "beauty" itself as an eternal verity, rather than a cultural construction.[15] We are told that the postmodern world has lost moral absolutes, but not so, it seems, aesthetic absolutes. The visual mass media have long been used to reinforce such absolutes, finding one powerful resource in the movie goddesses women are to resemble.[16]

Promises, Promises

In such a glamorized environment of possibility, or purchased perfection, marriage contracts that expect ideal mates may seem oddly appropriate. How different from the covenant we once imagined being made at the altar, the unconditional promise of endless devotion that now has a quaint ring to it. Still, there is a reason we cry at weddings and why actual marriage vows can never be boring. We cry because we see and hear people making promises they cannot possibly keep. But by faith they make them anyway. And by God's grace, if they stick through the humiliation and pain caused by the frank recognition of human inadequacy that marriage reveals, they sometimes grow into people who *can* keep such outlandish promises. Even Nietzsche claimed that the strength of any civilization rests in its ability to keep its promises. However, the sort of "promise" being made at the Cal-type wedding is so consumer driven, it might be perfectly at home in men who later leave their wives for younger women.

We can thank entrepreneurs like Hugh Heffner for the redefinition of manhood that inevitably accompanies this willingness to break faith. In its formative years, the editorial content of *Playboy* magazine was so antimarriage that men who "just read it for the articles" probably posed the real threat to domestic happiness. A central message in those early issues was that marriage hijacked the good things from a man's life—those things being money, freedom, and pleasure—and replaced them with a domineering freeloader called a wife—the old ball and chain.[17]

The pornographic images in *Playboy* were simply building upon the idea that sex could and should be purchased on an individual basis, and should not involve any kind of partnership and commitment, much less any form of sacrifice. A man was not a man because he could support a family. To the contrary, a man who was spending his income on a family was no man at all. A real man was a sort of boy, a playboy, armed with martini shaker, stereo system, and tiger skin couch upon which to conquer one female after another. Hefner was building on a proud tradition. During the gold rush, prostitutes outnumbered "respectable" women twenty-five to one.[18]

Both the advertising and pornography industries chop humans into body parts and invite us to consume that product as we would a tenderloin steak, without regard for the possibility that a person with a soul lays at the end of that protruding thigh. The notion of a spiritual transaction is out of the question in such an environment, and we would never expect it. Yet, we somehow expect to be freed from these thought patterns when we sleep with real people, and certainly when we've married them. How does that happen?

Stanley Cavell has identified a genre of screwball romantic comedies from the 1930s as "the Hollywood Comedy of Remarriage," in which he includes *It Happened One Night, Bringing Up Baby, The Philadelphia Story, His Girl Friday, Adam's Rib, The Awful Truth,* and *The Lady Eve.*[19] An important characteristic of these films is that the protagonists reunite with the same people they rejected earlier. What happens in the transformation from the first union to the second is an important subject. The characters rarely become much better people; but they are seen differently. Rather than being blinded by love, true (or more accurately, *truthful*) lovers are given far better vision.

The dissolution of relationship in these films is usually the result of too rigid a standard, allowing a marriage partner to "spiritually carve [his wife] in half, taking the good without the bad, the lady without the woman, the ideal without the reality, the richer without the poorer," in the words of Cavell, who adds, "He will be punished for this."[20] Similarly, when we allow ourselves to be duped by cinematic, corny, phony tales in which one perfect person finds another perfect person with whom to share a perfect life, that too will cost us something.

Historically, mistaken identities are a staple of comedies, particularly romantic comedies. Yet writers like Preston Sturges offer another spin. In *The Lady Eve*, one's identity can be mistaken, that is misunderstood, merely by the perceptions of another. We are all bound to mis-take one another's identity when we assume the worst about each other, when we think we know a person better than we do, or when we don't allow that person to be human, as they were intended to be. Paradoxically, the only way to identify a person accurately is to trust him or her *before* we know everything, and thus to make ourselves vulnerable. This requires faith. When we decide to make judgments based upon our woefully inadequate knowledge, without faith, we reenact the scriptural account of the fall of man daily. This is why the film credits of *The Lady Eve* feature an animated snake slithering madly in the garden of Eden.

Scripturally, marriage is a spiritual transaction. Adam *knew* Eve, not merely because he had a sexual encounter with her, but because he had a psycho-spiritual encounter. He understood her; he "got" her at the most profound level. And this knowledge happens only when we surrender what we *think* we know, that is, our judgment of each other based on our dull notions of perfection. If we'd stop trying to play the part of gods and goddesses, we might stand a chance at being decent humans. But in the Comedies of Remarriage, humans can only become good humans when they are forgiven for being bad humans—or forgiven for being humans at all.

The media make much of erotic scandals, but, writes Cavell, "what they mean by erotic scandals consists of triangles, crimes of passion, sensational marriages, and ugly divorces. What our films suggest is that the scandal is love itself, true love."[21] Likewise the scandal of a scriptural gospel that dispenses grace to the undeserving is that people can be made innocent, not because they are guiltless, but because they are forgiven. The protagonists in these films finally forgive each other for their humanity, and that is the *really* happy ending. For innocence is not the absence of sex, but the absence of guilt, such as one might experience in extramarital sex. Sex without the acknowledgement of a spiritual encounter, without the willingness to accept the human with whom we sleep when we wake up the next day, is always extramarital, even when we're married.

Perfectly Fine

An old cartoon features a customs officer saying to a traveler, "Welcome to California. Any imperfections to declare?" Again, we can thank Hollywood for one major perfection model, but average folks often feel even more freakish in Orange County, which is a fabrication of the ideal. There, where the sun god seems most lavishly worshiped, the weather beckons one and all to disrobe. Beach culture has conspired with commerce and science to create the "perfect body" of H. G. Wells's blonde Eloi, and California girls, like Barbie dolls (created in El Segundo, California, by a woman working for Paramount Studios), emerge as the quintessential, mass-produced icons of sexuality, attracting international worship.

Now, the fertility idols of most cultures, including prehistoric civilizations, have some parts of the body exaggerated (such as breasts) while other parts are ignored (such as faces). But in a wild deviation from ancient idolatry, fertility and procreation are not the Cal-type's ultimate focus here. If anything, the opposite is true. Fertility implies family, thus *generational activity* and even *maturity*, devoutly to be avoided. Procreation is not the point. Sex is. In fact, fertility gets in the way of sex. How odd the notion of a "problem pregnancy" might have sounded to a culture that could not imagine fertility, but only barrenness, as a curse.

"Sex and the Single Boomer: The New World of Midlife Romance," was the February 2006 cover story of *Newsweek* magazine. I imagine this new world is supposed to be good news. But briefly setting aside the notion that our news media might have had more compelling issues to cover in 2006, I wonder if midlife itself might possibly offer more compelling possibilities such as wisdom, strength, humor, protection, leadership, or nurture. I noticed when I was living in Kentucky that it was common for older, overweight women in bathing caps to be romping on the beach with their grandchildren. I cannot remember the last time I saw such a thing in California. Brian Wilson told us he wished they all could be California girls and we snapped to attention.

Yet my Illinois grandmother was the first to admit that even as a young woman, she was far less attractive than her future husband was, and my grandfather was quick to admit she was smarter and better educated than he, and possessed of higher character. She was in fact considered to be quite a catch, despite her plain looks. Looking back at photographs from their era, I notice that women were often less attractive than their husbands. The difference in our time and place lies not only in values, but also in acquaintance. My grandparents grew up together and were friends long before they were sweethearts.

They were acquainted with one another's strengths and weaknesses and backgrounds. They had some understanding of what they were in for. In California, a land of transplants and strangers, we have little to go on but looks, even if we'd prefer to be less shallow. I became intrigued with life outside California when I first visited my grandparents' town in Illinois. At the time I was twenty-seven and living in San Francisco, a place of very radical lifestyles. But in Illinois, I learned that people slaughtered and ate animals that were once pets. They lived radical lives rather than radical lifestyles.

There has been a steady cultural shift in our attention from life and death issues to lifestyle issues. In the 1980s, Americans learned to ignore "crappy issues like human rights,"[22] in favor of bigger game, namely, becoming the international top gun, both militarily and economically. Sadly, this trend seems to have continued, as year after year we've surrendered "boring" domestic issues of state to the military–industrial complex. However, we cannot agree nationally to this principle until we have agreed privately to it. What we value in our marriages, we will value in the voting booth. At our weddings, "oneness" is intended to describe unity, not individuality, and as long as there is any confusion on the issue, it will affect our attitude toward God and country.

The tension between domestic issues and newer, more exciting, action-packed calls of the wild is an old one in California. In 1850, an editorial noted that "unlike any other country in the world's history, California has not been drawn together by ties of kindred and relationship."[23] Early on, men living perfectly meaningful lives as fathers, farmers, craftsmen, and community builders dropped everything to scamper after the promise of gold and fame, often dragging families with them to scrounge and starve when the big gamble didn't pay off. "Frenzy seized my soul," one miner wrote. "Unbidden my legs performed some entirely new polka steps—houses were too small for me to stay in," too confining for "the fancies of my fevered imagination."[24] Even now, as we seek to gain our imagined lives, we can lose our real lives.

Smile, Please

How the Cal-type looks is so much more important than how we are, or what we are, or even that we are. Our children are the most photographed generation to date, but that's not their fault. Parents take the pictures. In much the same way that today's children are able to recognize a brand logo before they can recognize their own name,[25] children may know how to strike provocative poses and fake smiles before they know how to form friendships.

Photographs abound in California, particularly at the beaches. There, where it is often difficult to make eye contact with passersby, the one surefire icebreaker tends to be, "Would you like me to get a picture of both of you?" Because we are so habitually photographed, we are made aware of our looks. However, in Rome I had my picture taken among the ruins and I looked pretty ragged and it did not matter because the real story was about Rome. In California, folks rarely photograph historical "points of interest," only beauty, and in many cases, California's inhabitants need not be historically interesting, only beautiful.

I remember hearing that in certain African villages, natives were once fearful of being photographed because they believed the photo stole their soul away from them. For the Cal-type, the opposite appears to be true. We don't seem quite sure that we exist without seeing pictures of ourselves. Neither do we seem sure an event has been experienced unless cameras, both still and video, heavily document it. "You have been immortalized in film," early photographers used to tell their clients. Now we are "mortalized" by film as well. In the absence of our actual experience of life's events big and small, Kodak must provide evidence that we were there.

The theme of the 2005 Rose Parade was "Celebrate Family" and it had three floats centered on family photographs as opposed to family experiences. One float featured photographs mounted upon butterflies, the most ephemeral of creatures. All aspects were rendered in flowers, "living things," as the announcers reminded us, admitting their surprise that these "living things" had not marred the photographic images. Barbara Streisand's rendition of *Memories* played in the background. But in this context, memory is unstable and unreliable, slipping and sliding upon the surface of technology and pop cultural iconography.

History Is Nothing Personal

California is, historically, the most heavily subsidized state in the union. The federal government has bailed us out many times, almost as parents might treat the baby of the family. That sense seems to have played out in the lives of individual Californians who "did not so much grow up, then, as recycle their youth."[26] No matter what our actual age, California-ism seems intent that we be about nineteen. If we are younger than that, we need to put years on, and if older, we need to take them off, regardless of the psychological or physical costs. And if we do in fact age, we can still impose limits. "Forever 35," gushes a *Los Angeles Times* headline, as we giddily celebrate our mandatory holding pattern. We are not just a young state, we are a state of youngsters. Peter Sellars observes that Shakespeare's England was of a similar ilk as it began to adopt the values of an empire, and thus several of Shakespeare's plays deal with the question: will we survive our heady youth?[27]

Certainly, the obsession with youth is a nice setup for advertisers, since teens are the dream market targets. With target marketers determining our taste and then bombarding us with niche products, what better way to insure that we never change than to offer only one kind of thing the rest of our lives and not expose us to anything else, anything by which we might be further developed, enriched, or challenged? Anyone hoping to experience standard life cycles will have her work cut out for her.

The lack of really pronounced seasons in some parts of California creates the sense that our lives are lived in only one season, with minor variations throughout the months of the fiscal calendar in the fabrics we wear or the decorations in our homes. Our seasons are heralded by the new line at Hallmark, not necessarily the chirping birds, changing leaves, or falling snow (though Disneyland manufactures snowdrifts on Main Street in December). Bill McKibben observes that, for many, the word *season* has come to mean the new television season of programs, and he goes on to describe the debilitating effect on our psyches.[28] For when we are unable to learn from nature the lessons it teaches about birth, growth, full bloom, fruit bearing, and gradual death into the next cycle of birth, we sense that this process is somehow bizarre or grotesque.

In Southern California, as evidenced by the frequent lack of public transit and other community resources, we're not ideally set up for aging. "I always feel younger in California," a visitor told me. "It must be part of the ethos." He was right. During the gold rush in San Francisco, "it was difficult to find a man with grey hair."[29] California-ism seems to suppose aging is in mildly poor taste, primarily because it affects one's looks, but equally important, one's productivity, the ability to stay in the rollicking game of the good life. Aging in *Hollywood* is pretty much out of the question, on screen or off.

And so the Cal-type chases every form of youth possible, eternal springtime, and whether or not our inability to grow up stems from our own choosing or the demands of our culture seems impossible to tell. We're making up our own rules most of the time. We don't have the witness of nature's seasons to govern us as some places do, only our artificial images of change. In the same way that we cannot acknowledge death if we do not acknowledge life, we cannot know the revolutionary upheaval marriage brings upon our spirits, if we've not yet encountered our spirits.

William Blake describes a spiritual cosmology in which the seasons represent various aspects of the human spiritual cycle. In his account, Spring (called Beulah) is beautiful but vacuous and shallow. She has the innocence that results from naiveté, a lack of experience. Summer is languid and sensual, pregnant with possibility, and falling into temptation when she actually encounters the real world. Autumn is the tempestuous result—by turns revolutionary and repentant, overturning what has come before and longing for change. Winter is the aftermath of this chaotic revolution, brooding and still.

Symbolized by the character Urizen, a play on the words "Your Reason," Winter creates an introspection that can be deadly and paralyzing if one does not move on into rebirth, the new Spring that is no longer naïve. The resurrected Spring cannot bring herself to life, but must rely upon a force outside herself. Forgiven her past, she accepts new life, or true innocence as described by Blake. Scripture goes out of its way to insist we have no "natural" innocence, but must be reclaimed by a loving God and God's truly innocent Son.

California-ism encourages us to linger, not in a marriage for all seasons, but in a perpetual state of spring, without the changes the seasons should bring in order for us to grow spiritually. Instead, we hop back and forth between spring and summer, retreating when things become too hot, too real, too risky. The Cal-type can make occasional, splashy forays into autumn, but our revolutionary struggles tend to be political more often than spiritual. We can deny that we are tempted and that we fall and that we yearn and that we despair. But only our confession of these truths can pave the way for a genuine spring of rebirth: not a condition that *looks* innocent, but a condition that *is* innocent. California-ism allows us cheerfully to sidestep the whole process, staring into our mirrors as Beulah stared into the lake, checking to see if we're still here.

9

The Golden Chariot

Automobile Culture

"I hate California," Woody Allen quips in Annie Hall. "Their idea of culture is being able to turn right on a red light." But did he know how important that right turn could be? In September of 2009 as high holy days such as Yom Kippur and Ramadan are observed, San Bernardino will observe the nineteenth anniversary of "The Route 66 Rendezvous," a four-day event celebrating automobiles and automobile culture. During the heady days of early autumn, as harvest festivals gear up worldwide, California surf guitar bands and oldies radio stations provide background music for the engine-revving 2,481 hot rods and muscle cars (one for each mile of the route) that roar through the roped-off parade route downtown. Most of the entries are extravagantly cherried out, such as the GTO with columns of flames spiraling from its open header and the sleek Thunderbird with purple light throbbing from beneath the car body to compliment its translucent paint job. But other vehicles are simply old cars in disrepair, probably unable to pass smog inspection, and still proudly driven by neighborhood residents who made it into the lottery and are now waving happily to the unimpressed throngs of onlookers.

In addition to dangerous-looking corn dogs and rides for the kids, I have seen made-in-China automobile kitsch, fuzzy dice, neon signs, bowling shirts, tattoos, and tank tops available for purchase. Free stuff is thrown haphazardly into the fray, the residue of consumption that lies upon the land like a nuclear winter. A local paint store adopts the slogan, "Doing business since the automobile was young." Plastic Budweiser banners plaster the few remaining historic buildings downtown. The grayish sky is filled with grimy, gigantic balloon logos and makeshift pavilions for a fleet of corporate franchises. Faded celebrities act as parade marshals and sell autographed headshots. Smog and smoke and unyielding exhaust fumes combine with the epic heat of Indian summer to create a giddy sense of doom. Within this pounding environment wanders a shoulder-to-shoulder crowd of spectators, some of whom would be deemed trailer trash by those who watch their stories exploited by daytime talk shows.[1] This is where mullets go to die.

Incongruously, a larger than life but otherwise realistic painting of Will Rogers looms up the side of a building, and Rogers's kind eyes and rueful smile seem to pronounce a kind of benediction on this wild congregation, these sons and daughters of Okies like himself. The roaming throng may represent, in the calculus of California-ism, the genetically inferior that never made it all the way to the ocean, something like the turtles of Galapagos. Now they are viewed warily as desert folk, H. G. Wells's Morlock peering at the blonde Eloi who reside in beach towns and Hollywood, just as the inland environment vaguely calls to mind the smoky, technology-ridden underworld from which those creatures emerge.

Like the segment of Israel left to wander on the outskirts of the Promised Land, many locals have concentrated solely on survival. Caught between two worlds, the one escaped and the one sought, the "undesirables" remained semimobile, without permanence, going from one affordable rental to the next and one dead-end job to the next. They are always traveling and rarely progressing. Some have lived in hope that their children would reach that territory of dreams and have continued to encourage steady overachievement. Some have lost faith, broken trust, gone wild, and capitulated to their baser instincts. Some have found ways to settle in the desert and carve out a highly successful living. All show up for the Rendezvous.

The first time the term *rendezvous* was used in the West, it referred to a yearly gathering of French trappers that would determine who among them had survived the elements and was still on his feet.[2] Survivors were expected to notify the families of those missing, or at the least, to acknowledge their disappearance. Those who now assemble in San Bernardino have survived the journey to California, and more importantly, they have survived California itself. They have disappeared from America's media landscape, from the country's popular stories, sometimes even from the concerns of the government sworn to protect them, but they have not disappeared from the land itself.

No, they are here, rejoicing amid the instruments of their mobility and their destruction, instruments that have poisoned their air, uprooted their orange groves, exploited their unfulfilled, cruel dreams, and furiously replaced folk culture and community with commodity culture and isolation. The previous year has seen scores arrested on freeways and scores slaughtered there in accidents. And still we celebrate the automobile. And in this celebration, the thousands who laugh and cheer and dance seem to be openly refusing annihilation and perhaps renegotiating what it is to be "alive" for another year. Our celebrations might act as noisy, haphazard rituals, the working stiff's Burning Man festival where we seek *kairos* in *kronos*.

Diggin' the Scene with a Gangster Lean

I watched the meticulous, loving strokes of guys polishing the gleaming chrome of their side mirrors one more time. Nearby, dozens of photographs, almost like baby pictures, depicted their automobile in various stages of development, and at various locations. Wow, I thought to myself, people here sure do have an unnatural relationship with their cars. Then I saw it: a fire-engine red El Dorado Cadillac convertible. My knees buckled and nearly gave way beneath me. There was no denying the sensation in my stomach. I had a crush on this car. I had great reasons. This was the car my godmother drove. Her name was Helen, like my mother's, but there all similarity ended. They had met accidentally when my mom nursed Helen's dying husband and comforted Helen, who knew how to repay a debt.

She adopted my family gradually then suddenly, in the words of Hemingway, becoming my mom's best friend outside the church and appointing herself our ad hoc godmother. Before we knew it, she was renaming my baby brother, dropping cigarette ashes on our carpet, overspraying cologne, and talking us into all kinds of craziness. Beside my mom's crisp uniform and conservative hairdo stood Helen, in backless stiletto heels with cherry clusters, gold lamé turban and dangly earrings, black velvet capris and rhinestone sunglasses, her lipstick and nails the same red as her car. I adored her. She was outrageous and exciting, and she scared and delighted us all. Helen bought me a pair of dress-up heels (also gold lamé) when I was seven years old, and a porcelain china tea set I displayed precariously on our radiator then watched fall to pieces when the radiator got bumped. It had been the most beautiful thing I'd ever owned and I wept bitterly as my mom reminded me she'd asked me to keep it boxed up.

I met Helen about the same time of my conversion, and the fact that she called herself my godmother I am sure had something to do with how I began to see God. Helen lifted us out of Colton and onto the beach on her magic carpet, the convertible. She sped us to the drive-in steering that same enormous vehicle. She sat with us on the bench seat to watch the movie screen suspended in the twilight and rocked with loud laughter at the opening cartoons. The El Dorado was, of course, more than a car. It was a promise. When Helen pulled up in front of our house and honked the horn, my stomach tumbled with anticipation. This would be an adventure—a day or night out of Colton that I would remember for the rest of my life. And sure enough,

I have. I remember when she took us into the San Bernardino Mountains during a forest fire so we could "see the action up close!" She told the police guarding the area that her husband was up there fighting the fire and she'd brought his lunch and we were their kids. The police actually let her pass. They asked her to put the convertible top up, which she did, lowering it again when we were out of sight. Flaming timbers fell to the right and left as she cried "Wow, kids! Ever see anything like this?"

I also remember when she crossed four lanes of traffic in Hollywood, swerving from the far right lane to the far left, hollering at the outraged drivers she endangered, "Oh, dear! I'm so sorry! This is where I need to turn! Thanks, guys! Thank you!" For a time, I thought she had purchased the convertible so she could yell explanations to the other drivers, she did so with such regularity. As it turned out, she didn't purchase the convertible at all. She borrowed the keys from an acquaintance and never brought the car back. Although she never would have called it grand theft auto, others did. A nice man who was desperately in love with Helen took the rap, for which she later married him.

It's easy to see why Helen terrified me even as I loved her. She was too loud, too kooky, too overwhelming, too dangerous, too reckless, too extravagant, too colorful, too exotic, too everything—and too nice to me. I had a hard time fully trusting her. She defied all assumptions about how the world worked. Not everyone loved Helen, but no one could ignore her. She was utterly, doggedly, unashamedly *alive* in the desert.

This, for me, is the great appeal of the Rendezvous. Out of the cheap plastic iconography that lampoons consumerism at its most pointless, out of the buzzing neon, the transgressions and threatened annihilation, Steinbeck's ill-fated Californian resurfaces gasping for air, still laboring at low wages, still waiting to reap the benefits of a territory to which we've sacrificed. At the Rendezvous, we are still alive. The sand has not swallowed us. Rolling down the Route 66 highway, we pretend we are still traveling, still headed somewhere, still contending.

So what if it's all over and the die are cast? We have dice of our own on our rearview mirrors. It's still not too late for one more chance. And we don't give a damn what others think of our tank tops and ratted hair. We're still here, beyond the reach of makeovers. If we're not wanted at the beaches, inlanders will gladly retreat to the desert hot springs, those places where our cellulite-ridden bodies are forgiven and welcomed. This kind of Californian won't dissolve into the white radiance of the celebrity beam. We can't possibly be assimilated. So if we wear halter-tops without having breast reduction surgery or grin without bleaching our teeth or dance without any particular talent, come and get us! By the grace of God, and despite the gracelessness of man, we're still alive, and where there's life, there's hope. I stand in the midst of the Rendezvous, and I smile and smile.

The Janis Joplin look-alike, sound-alike vocalist prances across the stage before her band and cries out, "Janis lives!" And here at the Rendezvous, she lives indeed. She is the queen of the underclass, the outcast of her Texan high school who wrote outlandish poetry and drank too hard and draped herself in feather boas and other parodies of high fashion. She screamed her laments to both those who listened and those who didn't. She told us she had nothing left to lose, so, like Godmother Helen, she personified freedom. She became our own William Wallace, encouraging the tattooed dispossessed, and clamoring for freedom, for justice, for expression, for our own little spit of property, for the promises made and broken. Oddly, the spirit of free-wheeling bohemianism expressed in the howling poetry of California's beat movement, the howling psychedelic music of California's hip movement, and the just plain howling of the Burning Man Festival (another California invention) are more alive here than among the corporate sophisticates currently residing in San Francisco, the birthplace of such movements.

The allure of such movements was in fact what drew me to San Francisco. There was something thrilling in the psyche-delic colors that pushed their way through the gray cocoon of dull conformity and cracked the cultural chrysalis into a million tiny pieces. The Cultural Revolution promised freedom in the same way the auto had. Mobility, personal expression, equal access to the American landscape regardless of race or gender—all these lay just around the corner. The Civil Rights movement, the Peace movement, the Women's movement—all that *movement* hearkened a grand future. But, as with the auto, freedom began to be equated with license in the public mind, and sometimes even in the public record. I think of the line in *The Big Lebowski*, when the Dude confronts the smug power broker who has derailed his life. "Your revolution is over, Mr. Lebowski. The bums lost. The bums will always lose."

Almost immediately, the political and philosophical gains of that vibrant, unwieldy era became enmeshed in the mass-produced glop that accompanied it. Peace medallions littered department store sales bins next to tie-dyed headbands, and at Halloween, little kids donned hippie costumes as I once had the costume of a Beatnik. Wow. Had my family, or anyone in my neighborhood, a clue about what the Beat movement was really about, that black beret and turtleneck I wore in the Lincoln Elementary School Halloween Parade would have been burned. But the well-oiled cultural hegemony that has continued to hum through one threatened political upheaval after another, quickly drains all such movements of their original meaning, making them seem corny and old fashioned. That includes even such significant activities as war protests.

The Mother Road: Road of Migrations, Vacations, and Incantations

There was a time when social service agencies showed *The Grapes of Wrath* to would-be immigrants in an effort to discourage their naïve belief that America (particularly California) held unlimited opportunities. But they were surprised by the response. Rather than focusing on the Joads' terrible poverty and suffering in the New World, viewers were unexpectedly impressed by their good fortune. After all, they owned a car. The conventional thought was that if a single family could have an automobile to themselves, regardless of its condition, they couldn't be that badly off. The automobile continued to represent many unrealized possibilities during the Depression, and Route 66, the Mother Road, became the yellow brick road that would lead the way to fulfillment. Unfortunately, early travelers found the dangerous road trip an ordeal more often than an adventure.

Then came the war, and after, postwar technology, with the postwar automobile perched at the very top of American affluence. Air conditioning and safety features meant a family could take a road trip based on choice rather than necessity. As is so often the case, dreams of a better life became desires for a better lifestyle. Route 66 glimmered and beckoned once more, becoming a symbol of prosperity rather than desperation, and up sprang the roadside attractions, novelty food stands, motels, and repair shops so richly commemorated in the animated film *Cars*. But Hitler wasn't the only one who could build a freeway, and with the introduction of the major interstates, the old road petered out, except in the ongoing imaginations of adventurers everywhere. Route 66 clubs are an international phenomenon, from France to Japan. Lauded in story and song, Route 66 is one of the few remaining historical roadways in California. My neighboring city of Glendora renamed Foothill Boulevard "Route 66," and my own university in Azusa still maintains the marquee from the last drive-in theater on Route 66 in California, now part of our west campus.

But the Route 66 Rendezvous is unique in its attentions to the Mother Road, and the cars from the '50s and '60s at the Rendezvous evoke more troubling images of a postwar era that we just sort of pretend to have survived. The Second World War effectively redefined America—its value systems, popular culture, art and education, the nature of family and sexual boundaries, and the roles of women, ethnic minorities, the disabled, and other marginalized groups. It would even redefine war itself. Some believe the very American psyche was altered. So, despite the well-scrubbed image of the 1950s wistfully invoked by those recalling "simpler times," it was actually a society in great stress and sudden, strenuous change.[3] Because this upheaval operated beneath a more stabilized or normalized surface, the hegemonic activity of the automobile industry becomes all the more meaningful.

Emblematic of so much more than the rampant enterprise and mobility increasingly identified with the American way,[4] the automobile became our own golden calf. The idol erected by the impatient Israelites in the desert was taken from the bull that provided transportation for Baal. It was a symbol of power, just as horses became during Solomon's reign. According to Walter Brueggemann's *Prophetic Imagination*, such mind-sets are in direct opposition to the "alternative community of Moses," which is built upon a vision of God that engenders true freedom, true energy, true promise and possibility, and true journey making. These are all the things the auto seems to offer, but never truly delivers. Instead, as to any empirical idol, we have sacrificed to the automobile time, money, landscape, infrastructure, culture, the air we breathe, human life.

Umberto Eco writes, "For the Californian, leaving his car means leaving his own humanity, consigning himself to another power, abandoning his own will."[5] Rather than waiting around in the desert for the will of another, even if the other is God, we, like Israel, seem determined to find our own way out. And as we speed off, if the law is broken, we'll just look out for cops. Our cars are not mere conveyances; they transport and transform our spirits. As Marshall McLuhan put it, our cars become extensions of ourselves. Transformation becomes a major metaphor at the Rendezvous. After all, these cars have been restored. Many had lain in ruin, passed over, like so many of the folks in San Bernardino. Yet now they are gorgeous new creations, their competition trophies and crowns displayed on the altars of their trunks. Sometimes Bible verses are written on placards near the cars, and sometimes religious artwork is part of the paint job. A church service might be conducted on the street with vaguely Christian lyrics set to Beach Boys songs. The year Pat Boone was Grand Marshall of the Rendezvous, his devotional books were sold in one pavilion.

The transparent lacquer that catches light and holds it, now used to paint so many of these autos, was originally developed in fifteenth century Italy for the making of icons, "to paint the body of Christ as a physical being filled with light."[6] Art scholar Dave

Hickey explains, "After World War II, Chicano car-cultists in the American Southwest began secularizing this central, sacramental metaphor, creating gleaming iconic automobiles that embodied, not the Word of God, but the freedom and promise of effortless mobility."[7] From then on, Hickey adds, "The emblem of the automobile as an embodiment of the promise of America—as an icon of Life, Liberty and the Pursuit of Happiness—would permeate the entire culture, Catholic and Protestant alike."[8]

He also explains that, in order to get people to keep buying new cars, a kind of spiritual hierarchy was created whereby "the consumer moved up the status-ladder within the cosmology of General Motors products." The company encouraged customers to "make incremental steps up the price ladder, as that exquisite, finny grail [the tailfin] gradually descended toward their aspiring spirit."[9] I recall an automobile commercial from years ago that introduced the company's new trinity—three new car models that rose to the skies together and disappeared into the heavens.

Backing into the Future

The glamour created by the Hollywood cowboy and other heroes of the West, prompting our desire to be independent and free-riding loners, turned on us with a vengeance. Loneliness once seemed "a kind of cultural inheritance, with our lone ancestors, the hunters, the trappers, the frontiersmen, all of whom lived a life of relative isolation and bragged about it." Now "drivers look as though pursued by an inner loneliness, hurrying some place but never knowing where that place is," writes Rollo May. "Their expressions have a forlorn quality, as though they had lost something—or rather as though they were lost," or even "pursued by guilt." What is missing is "a sense of peace—quiet, deep, relaxed peace."[10]

The new life promised by the automobile never really played out as expected. "Drive Less. Live More," reads the highway sign inviting drivers to try a new toll road. Like Travis Bicknell in *Taxi Driver*, we've begun to feel entombed by our cars. Many automobiles are no longer the sexy vehicles that fueled our deep desires. They are overpriced, underperforming pods, often resembling the stark white, charmless vehicles of the Star Wars Empire. They ensnare us in traffic, encumber us with endless, friendless commutes, and keep us reliant on foreign oil. They may ruin us. So, what happened? According to Hickey, one thing that happened was that the creativity once devoted to the automobile was devoted instead to advertising once it was determined that desire was a commodity in and of itself. Thus, we just started buying images certain brands evoked.[11] The myth of the New Land, we might say, was replaced by the myth of the New Product, the ultimate promise of advertising.

American businesses had long since stopped "advertising products for what they were, or for what they could do" and instead, marketed them for "what they meant as sign systems within the broader culture,"[12] perhaps ultimately, within the eternal realm. "American commerce began creating finite sets of objects that embodied ideology for a finite audience frozen in time, creating desire rather than fulfilling needs."[13] So, we think back. When was the last time we Americans felt good about car culture, or for that matter, anything else? We guess it was around the 1950s. And once again, the 1950s come to represent the dawn of time. Let's return to the '50s, just as Marty McFly must in *Back to the Future*. He travels by car, a nuclear powered DeLorean. We should too.[14] Let's go back like Marty and fix what went wrong. My goodness, we had it made, didn't we? We were going to create space travel and world peace! What on earth are we doing now, in the first decade of the twenty-first century, once again facing the possibility of global annihilation? Let's go back, okay? Let's look for sustainable energy after all. Let's take care of the environment, as our second grade teachers urged.

This return to the beginning of the world as we now know it follows an ancient principle, a principle associated with "sacred time." According to historian Mircea Eliade, "Sacred time is . . . primordial mythical time made present,"[15] tied to a sacred event that took place in a mythical past, "in the beginning." Life without car culture is nearly impossible for most of us to imagine, and the postwar mass production of the auto constitutes a "beginning."[16] I think again of the sign on the San Bernardino paint store: "Doing business since the automobile was young."

In many ways, I believe the Rendezvous acts as a primordial festival, with its sweaty revelries, its fire and smoke, its exhaust pipes roaring out during harvest season upon what was once agricultural land. Eliade observes that "what is essential is periodically to evoke the primordial event that established the present condition of humanity."[17] We do this, as ancient pagan cultures have, by re-creating the devices of the gods: in the case of the Rendezvous, their transportation. I remember saying to my husband that a certain muscle car looked like a boat, but I admit I wasn't thinking about Eliade, who makes reference to the boats of the gods—the boats they teach men to make, or repair, or restore. In his words, "the object repaired" in the ritual event ceases to be a mere object and becomes "a mythical archetype—the very boat that the gods manipulated in [sacred time]."[18] Mythic time, such as that experienced in the yawning hours of the Rendezvous, cannot be confused with history, which is composed of a series of days in chronological time. To restore a car is to travel to the beginning.

Sacred time is born and reborn, representing new beginnings, new chances to get it right—no jammed freeways, no smog, no blighted scenery or crass commercialism of billboards, no international implications, no dire consequences, just the original car—and always the car associated with one's youth and with obtaining a driver's license, perhaps the only shared rite of passage in America. Instead of the Bar Mitzvah (or Bat Mitzvah), during which one enters adulthood as a son or daughter of "the Word," most of us enter the on-ramp armed with our deadly automobile. "Now I can get a life," I heard my son say upon receiving his license, and I smiled remembering a time when I actually *wanted* to drive. "Nostalgia for origins is equivalent to a religious nostalgia for paradise," writes Eliade.[19] Nostalgia is not only encouraged at the Rendezvous; it's practically required. "The participants in the festival become contemporaries of the mythical event. In other words, they emerge from their historical time—that is, from the profane time constituted by the sum total of personal and intrapersonal events—and recover primordial time, which is always the same, which belongs to eternity."[20]

"Oh, I'd never drive this car for everyday," the proud owner of a 1957 turquoise Chevy at the Rendezvous tells me. "This is for once in a lifetime occasions." The car only operates in sacred, mythological time. The problem is, pollution operates in profane, historical time, as do all the other woes unleashed by the automobile. And it occurs to me that the historical results of our cars have not been truly *real* to us—perhaps because we do not realize our cars travel in real space and time. After all, we measure distance, not in miles, but in time. "I'm about forty minutes away," I'll tell my friend. I have no idea how many miles that is. Am I even traveling through actual territory? Or as in the video games, am I merely transversing hyperreality? I'm ever more intrigued by the way in which young drivers, especially, operate their vehicles at the same speeds and patterns as video games, flying up to the rear of another car and tailing closely until a tiny gap emerges through which to slip, stealthlike. Why not take the risk? It's not as though this is real life.

In our souls, we may sense that in trying to prolong the age of cheap oil we are stuck in a superstitious holding pattern. Our imaginations may manage to convince us for one more year that the social and economic turmoil created by our choices can be cleansed away by rites of our own making. Things can be made right again. *We* can be made right again. Simultaneously, we can carouse and careen and endlessly confuse license with freedom. However, in this quasi-religious pursuit, whether we are breaking the law or obeying the law, the emphasis is on the *law* rather than the gospel. My mother, Helen the rule keeper, and my godmother, Helen the rule breaker, were two sides of the same coin. Behavioral prisons or prison breaks never leave room for the full pardon of grace, and that's a serious religious trap. We can turn right on a red light, all right. But we can't get out of the car.

10

East of Eating

Food

It seems I awoke from a deep daze the year I turned seven, and I'm sure it had much to do with my conversion. It is hard for me to believe, even now, how much was lost on me before that. I was about that age when I sat in the movie house, watching a scene in which a bad guy was on the run from the cops. In midflight, the villain entered the home of an innocent family and inexplicably began to grab food from their table and gnaw at it.

"What's he doing?" I asked my big sister.

"Eating," she hissed.

"Why?" I continued nervously, knowing the cops were gaining on him as he sat working on a biscuit.

My sister rolled her eyes. "People have to eat, Monica. Be quiet!"

Something awful took hold in a section of my brain as yet, remarkably, untouched. I shuddered, partly owing to the apprehension churning within me and partly in fear of my sister's temper. The criminal on the screen now chomped at a chicken leg under the disapproving gaze of the neatly coiffed screen housewife, who bit her lip. I could stand no more.

"How come?" I demanded.

My sister turned her full force upon me. "People die if they don't eat! Okay?"

My head fell back on the movie seat, and I mouthed, "What?" I stared at the villain on the screen, who looked over his shoulder and swallowed food faster and faster. I'd never felt so sorry for anyone. How could I not have known that we ate because we *had* to eat? In my mind, people got hungry because they'd been working and playing, and we ate so we could keep working and playing. But I had no idea people were so completely vulnerable—even bad guys, tough guys. No matter who we were, or what we were, people were all in the same terrible boat. We needed food in order to live.

Looking back, it's hard to believe how heartbroken I was the afternoon I left that movie house. Sure enough, the villain had been mown down by gunfire from the cops, all because he'd had to stop to eat. I shook my head all the way home from the New Colton Theater, mourning for him, mourning for humanity, the real humanity with whom I'd so recently become acquainted. After that, I actually heard my mother the first time she said, "Finish your dinner. Other children are starving." And I shoved fish sticks into my mouth with the fervor of an evangelist.

Just Desserts

Later, I realized we weren't supposed to root for the movie criminal, but to understand that he'd gotten what he deserved. He had added to his other crimes the theft of these good people's hard-earned meal, threatening the family and messing up their dining room along the way. He needed to keep moving, not only for his own sake, but also for theirs. Should anyone be expected to feed someone so clearly undeserving?

The current global food crisis is creating a pressing issue with dire consequences.[1] Who deserves to eat? At first glance, this bizarre question may seem foreign and barbaric to us. But as is true of so many things, the American meritocracy embraced and perfected in California pulls this mind-set into our own backyard, literally. I think of the area once known as the South Central Farm in Los Angeles. (As a side note, the story of Los Angeles is far from over, and there is much reason to be hopeful. But in a city called literally "The Angels," we have reason to ask ourselves, what *kind* of angels? For Los Angeles is a city of spiritual, as well as social, extremities, and it is often difficult to identify the source of any given conflict. One simple source is money, but money itself is symbolic of something more— something more disturbing, I think.)

Consider this story. In the mid-1980s, fourteen acres of derelict property lay in the midst of South Central Los Angeles.[2] Former businesses had abandoned the district and in their place lay concrete pieces of foundation, discarded appliances, furniture, tires, rag piles, garbage, broken glass, and all the other refuse that ends up in the neglected parts of crowded cities. Rats and other vermin were the sole occupants, and they had a field day. The city needed a place to build an incinerator and its leaders decided this neighborhood of warehouses and factories provided a suitable site. No one seemed to notice that there were also homes in the neighborhood, for these belonged to the poor and powerless, and rarely raised much concern. Thus, in 1986 the space was expropriated by eminent domain for a little under five million dollars from nine companies, the largest of which had owned just over three quarters of it.

Then the first unexpected thing happened. The folks living in the neighborhood voiced their disapproval of the construction of a city incinerator in their backyard. Years of protests followed, and finally, in the wake of the Los Angeles riots of 1992, the city altered its plans. Those fourteen acres were made available in 1994 to the Los Angeles Regional Foodbank, housed directly across Alameda Avenue from it. The Foodbank in turn offered it to its neighbors, who embarked on the laborious task of clearing the land of the debris with the remarkable intention of cultivating the land. They then carted in fertilizer to rake over the emerging soil as well as plants and trees to grow there. It was an enormous effort, undertaken before and after long hours at other workplaces. But a decade later, there appeared in the middle of South Central Los Angeles (one of the most shredded neighborhoods in recent US history) perhaps the country's largest urban garden. And it was gorgeous. The California sun had worked its magic.

There's Spoiled, and Then There's Spoiled

I well remember one of my more embarrassing moments as a resident of Kentucky. Upon my first visit to the local market, I found a crate of small, brownish oranges, another of wilted lettuce, another of squishy tomatoes, and so on. Nothing looked edible. Finally I asked the grocer where the produce was kept, and he pointed in the direction of the crates. I heard myself say, "Oh, I'm sorry. I meant the regular produce," just as it was dawning on me that these crates of "rejects" were in fact the entire produce section. The grocer shot me a withering glance. Evidently rudeness in Kentucky is at least as scandalous as a poor selection of citrus.

I still blush over the incident, but for my sake, I'm glad it happened. Throughout history, "California's plant life has consistently mocked conventional notions of abundance and scale."[3] No wonder I'd see people from other states taking pictures of the produce at Farmers Market on Beverly Boulevard, instead of looking for movie stars. The food itself was the spectacle. From this perspective, the mythic artwork found in California postcards and crate labels seemed more than appropriate. This produce must indeed appear to be the nectar of the gods that humanity has pursued since the beginning of recorded time. Unfortunately, some may reason that, by extension, such delights are not intended for ordinary humans—which brings us back to the South Central Farm.

There, California's endless growing season conspired with the dedicated labor of men, women, and children, largely of

Mexican and Mesoamerican descent, to grow over a hundred species of nutritional and medicinal plants. Lugging buckets of compost and water, families worked shoulder to shoulder

> breathing air cleaned by the leaves of stalks rooted in new earth and rising toward the brownish gray city sky, children running down paths between garden plots, playing, dancing, making the mischief and art children make, their mothers, fathers, and grandparents with dirty boots, knees, and hands working, sometimes laughing, sometimes angry, sometimes distraught, usually simply on task. Corn, potatoes, chiles, cilantro, cactus, onions, tomatoes, tomatillos, agave, yams, sugarcane, beans, alfalfa, mallow, chamomile, purslane, quintoniles, and more grew in rows or beside them. Plots were dotted with avocado, walnut, banana, guava, and other fruit and nut trees [and eventually] a blighted neighborhood came to life, blossomed into a heavy fabric of the work and stories of impassioned people—a parable of hope, if ever there was one.[4]

Rufina Juarez, an elected representative of the farm, provided an eloquent description of the community that existed there at the turn of this century, when the farm was thriving.

> This place was opened every day from sunrise to sunset. . . . When we started organizing more . . . we would ask people, "Well, okay, it's the Fourth of July, should we close down?" They were, like, "No! We have no other place to go to!" [We'd ask,] "You know, it's going to be Thanksgiving, do you guys . . . ?" "No!" "Well, what about New Year's Eve?" And then they said, "No, let's open and close early!" Why? Because you have no other place to go! . . . This is their only place, this is the place. They didn't want to be stuck in their apartment, probably sharing rent with other families; they needed a space. . . .
>
> We had the best meals, the best times, the best music . . . dancing. . . . And underneath . . . the walnut tree we would have the services, the Christian service, the Catholic service. . . . [At] one of the [worship services] . . . we introduced two crosses, one for the north and one for the south. A farmer made them out of wood, real plain. And then we would rotate them, because there

was mass once a month and then you would take care of that cross, take it to your house for prayer and worship and then you would bring it [to the next service] and then that person would bring some food, because that's the tradition: eat with everybody. . . . That is, I think, what makes up a community: how you pray, how you play, where you live, where you eat. . . .

[At the Farm] faces were happy, because they were working the land and growing a plant and cleaning and weeding, like they were so much at peace with themselves. In the middle of all this bad violence, in the middle of this concrete and contamination there was this little, little peace . . . like they were really one with, well, the Creator, one with the Creator.[5]

About the same time, as the property began to gain high financial value, partly due to the opening of the Alameda Corridor,[6] there appeared on the scene a developer who claimed rights to the property. He was a partner of the company that had previously owned most of the property the city acquired in 1986. He argued that when plans to build an incinerator were abandoned, he by law had had the right to buy back the land. Early on, the city denied his claim, but in 2003, in a session closed to the public, and one that cost taxpayers dearly, the city agreed to the sale. "He once more acquired the land for about $250,000 more than the city had paid for it seventeen years earlier. Adjusting for inflation, the 2003 purchase price was equivalent to over $3,000,000 *less* than what the city had paid, that is, in 2003 dollars."[7]

It was rumored that at one time this landowner and developer was negotiating to replace the South Central Farm with textile-industry tenants—including one accused of sweatshop practices; and later, that he planned to sell the land for warehouse storage by large retailers such as Walmart. As of this moment, I don't know what will become of the property. I only know it is no longer a farm. To replace this farm—where children found the only safe place in the neighborhood to play, where neighbors met one another often for the first time, offered their food and ate together, talked, prayed, sang, and danced together (perhaps because they ate together)—with one more bleak warehouse in South Central may seem to constitute as much irony as this story can provide. But stick around.

After farm advocates waged a long, highly visible battle with its new owner,[8] a battle heroic to many, he finally agreed to sell it to the farmers (minus about two and a half acres) for the staggering sum of sixteen million dollars. Needless to say, the farmers didn't have that amount of money. However, charitable nonprofit organizations miraculously raised the finances, following a popular grassroots movement, and there was great public rejoicing. Los Angeles seemed to have found its soul. It was operating on the side of the (heavenly) angels. Then out of the blue, the owner refused to accept the offer, claiming that he had been the subject of public insults and character assassination, though little specific evidence could be provided. Evidently, the important thing was to make the case that the farmers did not *deserve* the land, whether or not it could be purchased for them by a hopeful and believing populace.

This Land Is My Land, Mister Guthrie

The attitude that agricultural California is a land reserved for a deserving, elite class is deeply entrenched in Southern California's history and dates at least as far back as the "orange rush" of the late nineteenth and early twentieth centuries. Gentlemen farmers from across the nation, attracted in droves to the agricultural California of aforementioned postcards and crate labels, came to represent the "right" kind of landowner and citrus grower. Though expenses were high, as historian Glen Gendzel notes, "Orange-rushers were undeterred by the hefty price tag of their dream because it guaranteed that their new neighbors would be affluent Anglos like themselves."[9]

For Anglo would-be growers in southern California, this seemingly formidable barrier to market entry was a blessing in disguise. The substantial start-up cost of citriculture restricted the orange rush to prosperous participants who brought sizeable sums with them, ready to expend on arrival. Less-wealthy

Anglos could settle in modest bungalows with a few token orange trees in the yard, but working-class and nonwhite migrants
were welcome only to the extent that their presence increased
the cheap labor pool and kept wages low without depressing
property values. They would have to live invisibly some distance away from their employers. Only Anglo migrants who
could afford the high price of admission could share the fruits
of someone else's labor, the labor of those excluded from the
grower's lifestyle by barriers of race as well as class.

According to Gendzel, in 1894, the booster magazine *Land of
Sunshine* assured investors, "There is nothing wild and woolly
in Southern California, . . . It has filled up with educated and
well-to-do people; and . . . it will continue to fill up with the
same sort. . . . Barbed wire would not keep out the undesirable
classes, but the price of land will—$300 an acre is as tall a fence
as is needed around any community."[10]

Left out of the equation were Southern California's non-
wealthy, non-Anglo residents, "many of whom worked in the
citrus industry and whose presence in reality made possible a
fantasy defined in part by their imagined absence."[11] Eventually,
"the aggregated desires of these orange-rush migrants converged
to create a 'bourgeois utopia' dispersed into racially segregated
enclaves," as "the sheer mass of their collective presence began
making their individual dreams of an Anglo Eden come true."[12]
And, right on cue, the agricultural empire formed the age-old
argument: our dreams come true because we are better people
than most. Charles Fletcher Lummis, editor of *Out West* magazine, went so far as to create a spiritual distinction between
southern Californians and their northern brothers. According
to Gendzel,

Anglo Californians of the north might consider themselves children of the [Gold Miners], but Anglo Californians of the south
did not. These new arrivals hailed from the rural and small-town
Midwest, not the urban East or foreign lands; they rode west in
railroad cars, not in sailing ships or covered wagons; they lived
in flower-bedecked houses, not in rude canvas tents; they came

as families, not as men alone; they worshipped God, not Mammon; and, Lummis wrote with pride, "instead of gophering for gold, they planted gold."[13]

Thus drifted south the alleged meritocracy that enabled lucky (or larcenous) gold mining companies to credit their superior personal character as the source of their bounty. Now lucky farmers (turned businessmen) claimed a meritocracy based on even *more* superior character. And as usual, those who were not lucky were those who, it was assumed, merited no luck. Those such as the South Central Farmers had to be made to appear deserving of their unfortunate fate, which was a harsh one indeed. Craig Keen describes it well.

> On the morning following Independence Day, 2006, the Los Angeles Sheriff's Department cleared the way for a crew that over the next two days systematically bulldozed the South Central Farm, destroying the fruit of over a decade of the sweat and pain and care of hundreds of the poor children of this land. A year later the acres lay untended. A perimeter fence locked the Farmers out, the seeds of their ravaged gardens stirring and sending out green shoots, which the City from time to time mowed down, leaving brown earth and stubble beneath the dust their tractors threw up.[14]

Members of the activist Cornerstone Theater arrived for one of many vigils held in the days before the farm was destroyed, and read aloud chapter 19 of *The Grapes of Wrath*.

> Once California belonged to Mexico and its land to Mexicans; and a horde of tattered feverish Americans poured in. And such was their hunger for land that they took the land—stole Sutter's land, Guerrero's land, took the grants and broke them up and growled and quarreled over them. . . . The Mexicans . . . could not resist, because they wanted nothing in the world as frantically as the Americans wanted land.[15]

I was there, and watched as dozens of farmers and their supporters listened raptly to Steinbeck's words. It was impossible to believe they'd been written sixty years earlier. As the smoggy sunset stung the eyes of those gathered, the next reader continued.

> Then, with time, the squatters were no longer squatters, but owners; and their children grew up and had children on the land . . . and crops were reckoned in dollars, and land was valued by principal plus interest, and crops were bought and sold before they were planted. Then crop failure, drought, and flood were no longer little deaths within life, but simple losses of money. And all their love was thinned with money, and all their fierceness dribbled away in interest until they were no longer farmers at all, but little shopkeepers of crops, little manufacturers who must sell before they can make. Then those farmers who were not good shopkeepers lost their land to good shopkeepers. No matter how clever, how loving a man might be with earth and growing things, he could not survive if he were not also a good shopkeeper. And as time went on, the business men had the farms, and the farms grew larger, but there were fewer of them.[16]

The listening crowd at South Central seemed to shift its weight collectively from one side to the other. The reader was cloaked in descending dusk, but her voice gained some intensity.

> Now farming became industry, and the owners followed Rome, although they did not know it. They imported slaves, although they did not call them slaves: Chinese, Japanese, Mexicans, Filipinos. They live on rice and beans, the business men said. They don't need much. They wouldn't know what to do with good wages. Why, look how they live. Why, look what they eat. And if they get funny—deport them. And all the time the farms grew larger and the owners fewer. And it came about that owners no longer worked on their farms. They farmed on paper; and they forgot the land, the smell, the feel of it, and remembered only that they owned it, remembered only what they gained and lost by it. And some of the farms grew so large that one man could not even conceive of them any more, so large that it took batteries of bookkeepers to keep track of interest and gains.[17]

Some listeners lowered their heads, and others stared up at the sky. Then the reader turned the page and Steinbeck provided a kind of answer. He described for us an enduring culprit, our propensity to value lifestyle over life itself.

[For] while the Californians wanted many things, accumulation, social success, amusement, luxury, and a curious banking security [lifestyle], the new barbarians wanted only two things—land and food; and to them the two were one [life]. And whereas the wants of the Californians were nebulous and undefined, the wants of [others] were beside the roads, lying there to be seen and coveted: the good fields with water to be dug for, the good green fields, earth to crumble experimentally in the hand, grass to smell, oaten stalks to chew until the sharp sweetness was in the throat. A man might look at a fallow field and know, and see in his mind that his own bending back and his own straining arms would bring the cabbages into the light, and the golden eating corn, the turnips and carrots. And in the south he saw the golden oranges hanging on the trees, the little golden oranges on the dark green trees; and guards with shotguns patrolling the lines so a man might not pick an orange for a thin child, oranges to be dumped if the price was low. [18]

Steinbeck's words now brought to mind those of Scripture: "An unplowed field produces food for the poor, but injustice sweeps it away."[19] The reader sighed and closed the book. It had become too dark outside to see.

May I Take Your Order, Please?

The loss of this symbolic battle for South Central speaks to larger issues, as does Steinbeck's warning about valuing lifestyle more than life itself. What happens to a culture that values cash over crops? How is it that so much rich land could end up in the hands of so relatively few, and that these few would have no particular love or care for it? Most troubling, if so basic a human need as food can be held ransom by the rich and powerful, what has the culture begun to believe about human worth? And what does it *believe* about food?

I recently directed a production of Steinbeck's soul-battering play, *Of Mice and Men*, and maybe that's another reason these issues nag at me. For despite the minivillains represented in that story, clearly the common enemy of all the characters is the "big land company" for which the field hands work and from which they continue to seek escape. Bucking barley becomes the major task of all the workers, as opposed to cultivating the rich variety of gardens and animals their imaginations seek. The workers are asking very little, according to Steinbeck, just a tiny patch of land and the freedom that is the alleged hallmark of California living. But not only are they denied this opportunity, they themselves are destroyed along the way. And their destruction seems both inevitable and arbitrary.

Steinbeck's writing reveals another spiritual dynamic in the state of California endemic to its character, one that gave us the gold rush, then the orange rush, and now the "food rush," or rather, rushed food. The fast-food industry that allowed for Ray Kroc's McDarwinism and swallowed so much of California's landscape whole ultimately revolutionized our eating habits, and thus, almost everything else about us. Echoing Steinbeck, Eric Schlosser writes in *Fast Food Nation*, "The early Roman Republic was fed by its citizen farmers, the Roman Empire by its slaves. A nation's diet can be more revealing than its art or literature."[20]

Schlosser describes the way in which young fast-food workers are both kept from their studies, which might ensure better paying and more meaningful jobs down the line, and kept from learning anything truly useful about food, for that matter. They do not grow and pick, as the migrant workers do. They manufacture burgers by number, package them by number, and ring sales by number. Meanwhile, work-related injuries and routine robberies of fast-food businesses make these youth unusually vulnerable. In 2001, Schlosser wrote, "Roughly four or five fast food workers are now murdered on the job every month," and "In 1998, more restaurant workers were murdered on the job in the United States than police officers."[21]

These human sacrifices go largely unnoticed in the drive-through, drive-by society of strangers who call their orders through voice boxes beneath a neon menu. Saint Paul wrote of a certain population, "their god is their stomach."[22] He is describing a people who are so alone, all they have are their appetites to keep them company. Gotta grab something fast and get back to work. Maybe I can work in the car while I'm waiting. What's taking so long? These people are morons! I gotta get outta here. I'll grab something later.

In this rat-eat-rat, dog-eat-dog social McDarwinism, if one is hungry, well, join the club! All Cal-types are hungry for *something*. But if we actually need to eat, shame on us. Where's that willpower by which one's worth is measured? The legends of California's anorexics whose character is calculated by what they *don't eat* might provide a compelling example of this perverse attitude toward so basic and ancient a need as food. As Sallie Tisdale notes, one's weight is now a symbol not only of one's personality but of one's soul.

"When I dieted," she writes, "I didn't feel pious just for sticking to the rules. I felt condemned for the act of eating itself, as though my hunger were never normal. My penance was not to eat at all."[23] As Jean Kilbourne observes, eating is equated with sinning. When a woman in a television ad says she was "bad" last weekend, what she means is that she ate a cookie.[24] The problem does not lie in our hunger, but in our humanity. It is our humanity that the empire will not tolerate.

Historically, the church has contributed to this vein of human deprivation, though it is far from biblical. The first recorded anorectic was a young nun, Catherine Benincasa, who in the eighteenth century lost her two sisters to death. She began to starve herself in an attempt to strike a bargain with God that would offer penance and protect the rest of her family.[25] To the extent that we seek absolute control over our bodies, our environment, and even over God's favor, we resemble this little nun.

Folks may read the Christian self-help book *Thin for Him* with the best of intentions, I guess, but the temptation lurking in the corner may be to somehow prove our spiritual superiority by dieting. And in this way, we both take our cue from California culture and confer back to it a limp pseudo-Christian blessing, as do the "Christian Beauty Contests" that have sprung up here and there. Such efforts inspire both ridicule and pity in a culture that occasionally may understand the basic precepts of Christianity better than the current church does. Authentic Christianity in fact makes us free to be mere humans, free to live simple, unsung lives contentedly, free to be vulnerable rather than powerful. Eating is a humble act, and eating in the presence of others, even more humble. When we accidentally spill something on our shirts, there's no escaping the moment. We are making public proclamation of our humanity, and must trust others to excuse us.

Designer Dining

The ideal cultural models do not eat at all. They *dine*, creating, directly and indirectly, that famous California cuisine: tasty, healthy, and often expensive. The powerful don't eat lunch; they do lunch. A scene in *Get Shorty* lacerates Hollywood's use of food to display one's importance when a film star played by Danny DeVito places an elaborate, lengthy, and detailed order for designer health food at a high-end restaurant, then gets up to leave when it is finally delivered. Food is an utterly abstract notion in this context. It constitutes an idea in our heads rather than a sensory reality.

The meals our eyes consume in magazines, Internet recipes, and televised cooking shows can never satisfy us; instead they operate as a metaphor of our desire, an arousal of our appetites. Thus Cal-types can become as polarized and schizophrenic in our food choices as we are in so many other consumer behaviors, vacillating wildly between "fat" and "lean" like the cows in Pharaoh's dream. Whether we fantasize about Big Macs or the cover-page salads featuring edible flowers, we remain locked inside our heads, devoid of sensory experience. When I teach my acting students the importance of sense memory, I remind them that they need to taste their food, really taste it, rather than merely consuming it. Results vary. One student reported that she stopped eating Doritos, others that they actually began to taste the chemicals in most of their foods.

According to Schlosser, smell matters more than taste to the fast-food industry. Our sense of smell creates instant memories that can, for example, associate fast food with comfort food and thus deliver cradle to grave customers, initiated with the Happy Meal.[26] "Scientists now believe that human beings acquired the sense of taste as a way to avoid being poisoned."[27] Yet, increasingly, we are discouraged from tasting our food. In 2001 Schlosser told us that the American flavor industry had annual revenues of $1.4 billion dollars and that about ten thousand new processed food products were introduced every year in the United States. No wonder natural food tastes funny to us. I think of the scene in *Lord of the Rings* in which Frodo's humanity is being drained as he approaches Mordor and the weight of the ring of power becomes heavier and heavier. The drain manifests itself in the fact that, not only can he no longer taste his food, he cannot remember what a strawberry tastes like.

The goals of Mordor are driven by technology, prompting us to consider another possible drain upon human experience, our own home appliances. In "The Machine in the Kitchen," author John Thorne describes the losses resulting from our capitulation to the solitary values of efficiency and speed in the form of the food processor and microwave. Our machines operate for us as slaves might, and with similar results. They do the work of preparing the food, but we are robbed of the experience. We are promised more leisure time as a result, time to read more magazines and Internet recipes, or watch more television, and time to perform the meaningless tasks of machine management, programming, and clean up.

Don't get me wrong. I am so happy and grateful that cooking is less laborious than it once was. Fighting through the heat and smoke in order to cook outdoors is rarely my idea of fun, as I keep trying to remind my barbecuing husband. But when it comes to modern conveniences, one must be careful not to reach a point of diminishing returns. "The devices making more

and more demands on our actual lived time do not themselves
provide experience to compensate for what they have taken away.
Instead, they provide a compressed, fictive experience that does
not take place in genuinely lived time."[28] Cal-types watch our
devices working, using our eyes again instead of our hands. We
are no longer part of the food preparation process, having surrendered the job to a literal "food processor," and, oddly, our
meals join the ten thousand "processed food products" being
introduced yearly. We may not be working in the kitchen as we
once did, but we might say we are being worked. As Thorne
observes, "To live, after all, is to experience things, and every
time we mince an onion, lower the flame under a simmering
pot, shape the idea and substance of a meal, we actually gain
rather than lose lived time."[29]

The thought patterns that make it seem more normal to manufacture food than to grow, tend, prepare, and serve it will be the
thought patterns we use to think other thoughts, as food becomes
ever less real to us. The health food movement is satirized in *Get
Shorty* not because it is not worthwhile, but because it distin-
guishes itself from the truly natural. A local farmer's market run
on local city streets and selling locally produced food of local
farmers is usually as natural as we need be. It is also affordable.
And it pulls us directly into the sensory experience of food, as
we smell fresh strawberries, shake out fresh celery, and sample
little pieces of fresh tomatoes, cheese, and homemade bread.

However, when local farms no longer exist due to the business
practices described earlier, other business interests will helm the
"natural food" industry. What is then produced is not necessarily
natural food, but designer food, another phenomenon deeply enmeshed in California's past. Though early writings on California
describe a fantastic land of larger-than-life food similar to the
grapes of Jericho, within this natural abundance Californians
still yearned to manufacture even more perfect food. One such
was Luther Burbank, who imagined "an utterly plastic botany"[30]
of engineered vegetables, fruits, and flowers. Food, like so much
else, is expected to perform for us, sort of like the dancing pears
and apples in the old "Fruit of the Loom" ads. Sure, the rest of

the world may salivate over any ordinary farmers market in the state, but here the Cal-type must strut impatiently and holler through our megaphones, is that the best we can do, people?

Designer food is not plucked and purchased with difficulty on the crowded, inconvenient streets of a once-a-week farmer's market. It is disarmingly packaged in suitably iconographic artwork and sold in the air-conditioned aromatherapy of holistic market chains. There, where spirit and food seem conjoined, we can be seduced into the last minute acquisition of a pricey yoga magazine as easily as we can the latest issue of *Women's Day* at any supermarket. But again, this is the agricultural temple of celebrities, containing the *real* nectar of the gods, the stuff that will make us live forever. And it requires nothing of us but money, and plenty of it.

Making Peace with Food

I'll be the first to admit these stores appeal to me mightily. But I believe that appeal has to do with the return-to-nature movement of my youth, so sadly co-opted and often, though not always, compromised. That instinct still reveals a basic, legitimate human longing and perhaps our best hunch as to human survival. The garden I seek to grow, without proper knowledge or preparation, conjures uneasy memories of the *I Love Lucy* episode in which Lucy bets Ricky she and Ethel can survive "naturally" longer than their husbands can. Of course, they fail, by, for example, baking bread of such incorrect yeast portions that it devours the kitchen, and so on. I fear equally catastrophic results, and in fact, have endured a few. But even though most of the cultural messages in my lifetime have told me that sustaining oneself organically and responsibly is a futile, corny effort, I still agree with Schlosser that how we eat says more about us than we can possibly imagine.

Scripture supports this view, and places enormous emphasis on food. It associates food with gladness and deep satisfaction.[31] Father Robert Capon remarks, "Food is the daily sacrament of unnecessary goodness, ordained for a continual remembrance that the world will always be more delicious than it is useful."[32] I think of my friend Jamie Jobb, who grows tomatoes so scrumptious that we can sit at his table all evening sampling different varieties and being surprised and delighted. I think of G. K. Chesterton's writings on fairy tales and the fact that the creation of a fictional "golden apple" is simply building on the wonder of a real, red apple, a thing that is in itself miraculous when regarded with fresh eyes.[33] And I think of my gardening buddies here at the university and the scores of home gardens, neighborhood gardens, community gardens, and urban gardens that have sprung up again and again throughout California and the rest of the nation.

The kingdom described in Christ's parables has nothing to do with starving, and everything to do with eating. The kingdom of heaven is often likened to some form of banquet, open and abundant. Christ is concerned when people are not eating. He risks censure by seeing that his disciples eat on the Sabbath, though it may involve "work." He performs his first miracle to ensure that a marriage feast can continue in full vigor. He provides a picture of God as the Father who feeds the "undeserving." Though Christ fasts and supports fasting as a spiritual enterprise, he utterly lampoons it as a display of religiosity. He goes so far as to fry fish for his disciples in his resurrected body!

Food is meant to make us not only happy, but also truly grateful. It is a means of grace. It strengthens and comforts, and it allows us to share hospitality and community with others. In fact the word "companion" means, literally, "the one with whom bread is broken."[34] Astonishingly, food becomes the means by which Christ's very presence is imparted through the sacrament of communion. Food appears to be a pretty big deal. But again, Christ means to make us free to be human. He was in fact crucified, in the view of the Roman Empire, as a way to destroy his humanity, the goal of all crucifixions. Empires have no room for humans. The kingdom does.

11

Choosing Life

Recommendations for the Future

The journey to this point of American history has been tumultuous, frightening, and exhilarating, as are all mythic journeys. In recent years, moving from the presidency of George W. Bush to that of Barack Obama, the country has shifted so dramatically from one end of the spectrum to the other that folks around the world are scratching their heads in wonder, despite what they might know about America's melodramatic tendencies. There were several memorable moments in the 2008 campaign season. But one that struck me personally involved Maria Shriver, who was, among other things, the First Lady of California.

The day she showed up to declare publicly her support for Obama, a last minute decision and a courageous one, she declared, "If Barack Obama were a state, he'd be California. Think about it: Diverse, open, smart, independent, bucks tradition, innovative, inspiring, dreamer, leader. And the thing I like the best, he's not about himself . . . he's about us." I thought to myself, Wow. California really is all that, or at least, could be. Meanwhile, Shriver continued, "Have a conversation with yourself. Ask, what kind of America do I believe in? Do I believe in an America that sees beyond the labels [that] divide us? Everyone

[here] can be an agent of change." She quoted the Hopi prayer, "We are the ones we have been waiting for." And she concluded, "Remember, so goes California, so goes the nation [sic]."[1]

In the early twenty-first century, California is in deep trouble, and sure enough, so is the nation. We have attempted too much with too little, and it may well be that a shift in perspective or values will be forced upon us: simplicity, sustainability, civic-mindedness, and responsibility (literally, the ability to respond)—all the corny, unsexy things academic "dweebs" and grassroots organizations have promoted for years. I think about America's thrilling, reckless, long-running binge of the Roaring Twenties leading to our last great financial crash, and the ways in which everyone, yet no one, saw this coming. Suffering from blurred vision and diminished capacities, we collided at high speeds with truth. "An unbelieved truth can hurt a man much more than a lie," writes John Steinbeck.[2] Now it's as though the court has remanded us to rehab and Americans may be forced to quit California-ism cold turkey.

Step one of our "sobriety program" is to *admit we have a problem* that must be addressed through spiritual means. We must attack the personal roots of that problem and begin to make amends with our actual environment and communities. Then, with the help of fellow recovering addicts, we must resist the temptation to binge on manufactured pagan mythology derived from man-made efforts to wrestle the divine into our tiny idolatries, no matter how grand they seem. Instead, we must throw ourselves upon the mercy of the higher power that provides the serenity and strength to live *real* lives in our right minds.

Like most of America, California is as wondrous a land as has ever existed. As I've noted, it is easily mythologized. But to occupy it well requires us to regain a sense of wonder and gratitude. This in turn requires admitting our simple humanity and even rejoicing in it, as we align ourselves with an absolute truth, beauty, and goodness beyond our understanding and certainly beyond our grasp. A reasonable place to begin this process is in the church, presently captivated by man-made, pop cultural exigencies, but retaining the possibility of obedient submission to orthodoxy—right worship—that God makes available through word and sacrament. Steinbeck had the sense to know that the crux of California's future lay in the Hebrew word *timshel*, meaning "thou mayest."[3] We *may* choose well. We're gifted with the ancient choice that man has been given from the beginning. We can choose life, as God hopes, or the slow death of addicts who have lost faith.

Steinbeck uses the story of Cain and Abel, "the symbol story of the human soul,"[4] as the root metaphor in *East of Eden*. The character Cal (Caleb, who entered the promised land) is tied to reality and to the actual California landscape, his home, in a way his brother, Aron, is not. Aron is considered the "good" son, but he occupies a constructed world of heaven on earth that Cal knows cannot exist. Cal is aware of his own human condition, and that there is evil in him that he confesses regularly. What he doesn't know is that he is also capable of good, and he will not learn this until the end of the story, when he returns in humility to his father's house. His love for his father is what will ultimately redeem him, as well as his acceptance of his father's forgiveness. And all this must happen in Cal's real life, the only life he has.

Aron will not endure, but Cal will. He will be the one to survive, to marry and have children, as Cain did. We are, Steinbeck reminds us, the children of Cain. We cannot pretend we are too good to need reclamation nor too evil to be reclaimed. "Virtue and vice were warp and woof of our first consciousness, and they will be the fabric of our last, and this despite any changes we may impose on field and river and mountain, on economy and manners. There is no other story," writes Steinbeck.[5] That story has unfolded spectacularly in California. Despite our best efforts and the endless distractions provided by reshaping our environment, ourselves, our history, and our neighbor, we are still left to face our troubled and troubling nature. Nevertheless, as Cal is reminded, our fate is not sealed by our nature, but by our choices.

Resisting McCulture

I have chosen life in Azusa, California, a Los Angeles suburb suffering from all the mishaps that plagued my home in Colton. It is far from glamorous. Over my lifetime, in addition to hobnobbing with the rich and famous in San Francisco and Hollywood, I have lived in nearly every resort location the state offers, including Palm Springs, Lake Tahoe, and Laguna Beach. Returning full circle back to a community so reminiscent of the Inland Empire was my version of choosing *The Matrix*'s red pill. Much of Azusa's natural beauty and rich cultural promise has been parceled into franchises and cubes of concrete, resulting in that same cultural glop that plagues so much of Southern California, and increasingly, the United States that have come to resemble it.

When my husband and I moved here, the average annual income of Azusans was thirty thousand dollars a year (borderline poverty in California). The average age was twenty-seven, as it is a largely Catholic, Hispanic community with early marriages and many children. Off and on, Azusa has shared the outcome of several other communities comprised of low-income, Spanish-speaking populations with little or no voice in determining either their own futures or the values of dominant culture. Inevitably, such communities can be sold to the highest bidder. But the Mexican American community may soon be a majority again in California, and political democracy will rest heavily upon the possibility of cultural democracy.

In this atmosphere, the Azusa Renaissance Project has been launched. Founded by myself, my daughter and son-in-law, and students or alumni of Azusa Pacific University, where I teach, the project hopes to be an investment in the city's living cultural heritage. It aims to entertain, educate, and inspire the people of Azusa by way of the arts and to serve the commonwealth by nurturing the expression of human creativity; cultivating connection, unity, and goodwill; and fostering an appreciation of the quality and diversity of local artistic accomplishments. We train community participants through various workshops conducted by volunteering students, faculty, and seasoned artists.

My reasons for this undertaking were deeply personal. I have made references throughout this book to my early childhood, and to a few of the traumatic events that characterized it. However, outside my conversion to Christianity, I've not described the cultural factors that redeemed my life. They are twofold: the public library and the public theater. Not long after I learned to read, I headed for the library basement, which housed the children's library. On that Friday decades ago, I spent several hours sitting on a small stool, reading. Then I began to gather other books that interested me, creating several stacks according to genre. Most were fairy tales. By and by, the librarian came to tell me it was closing time. I asked her if I could keep the books there until the next morning, when I'd return to read them. Then she said something astonishing. "You can check some of those books out and take them home if you like." I thought to myself, "What on earth? Have you seen my home?" Apparently, it didn't matter that my home was chaotic and dangerous. The public library really was public.

My encounter with public theater was even more serendipitous. I went with my sister to one of the only really charming locations in Colton, a place called Fleming Park, not coincidentally near the library. Both structures were highly traditional, belonging to a bygone era when civic life was cherished. The park had the only existing public stage in town, and that evening, the stage happened to host a production of "The Little Mermaid." I had never before seen live theater and I was completely entranced. It was hard for me to believe that human beings were capable of anything that beautiful, and the imaginative hope it created in me was both instant and enduring. I guess this was my first step toward acting, but the journey that landed me in Hollywood could not hope to compete with this first, magical encounter. I was spoiled for life, and it was only a matter of time before I would drag my students into something called the Azusa Renaissance, in the hope that many other children, traumatized or not, would enjoy that same life-changing encounter.

Student feedback suggests that it has been, for most, a life-changing experience—for themselves, at least. They have strengthened research and communication techniques, gained tremendous knowledge and skill in liberal arts, and have learned to share that knowledge and skill in service to others as teachers, creative artists, and scholars. The first years of the project have been really tough, but students endured through some rough productions without the necessary crews, resources, or training, for that matter. The successes of the project have been many, but I believe these successes matter less than the very effort itself. Students are living in the real California with their real neighbors and doing real things. They have temporarily abandoned their video games and their daydreams in favor of everyday life, and they are occasionally finding wonder in that experience.

They have learned that to undertake the meaningful development of civic identity without benefit of cultural underpinnings is a useless endeavor. Traditional culture reflects the past, enriches the present, and imagines the future. When art flourishes in a community, lives change. Storytelling, especially, is used to make sense of our experiences as well as to envision alternate scenarios from which to draw lessons and make decisions. We use our stories to reason the validity of public policy as well as to form moral arguments.[6]

In the absence of a venue from which to relate these stories, communities are bereft of the narratives that might help them negotiate as citizens. Instead, they become reliant upon such narratives of the corporate world as television programs, advertisements, and franchises, by which they are led to respond as consumers at best and addicts at worst. Thus, the creation of public policy becomes an ever more distant and meaningless enterprise as populations are encouraged to leave such matters in the hands of "experts" and to engage in their everyday tasks as servants of an exterior value system that may have little or nothing to do with their innate wishes. Cultural democracy is necessary in order to insure political democracy.[7]

The Real Culture Wars

Kenneth Myers has provided a useful model by which to compare and contrast the characteristics of traditional (indigenous) culture with those of popular (mass) culture.[8] These are as follows:

Popular Culture	Traditional Culture
Focuses on the new	Focuses on the timeless
Discourages reflection	Encourages reflection
Pursued casually to "kill time"	Pursued with deliberation
Gives us what we want, tells us what we already know	Offers us what we could not have imagined
Relies on instant accessibility; encourages impatience	Requires training; encourages patience
Emphasizes information and trivia	Emphasizes knowledge and wisdom
Encourages quantitative concerns	Encourages qualitative concerns
Celebrates fame	Celebrates ability
Appeals to sentimentality	Appeals to appropriate, proportioned emotions
Content and form governed by the requirements of the market	Content and form governed by requirements of created order
Formulas are the substance	Formulas are tools
Relies on spectacle, tending to violence and prurience	Relies on formal dynamics and the power of symbols (including language)
Aesthetic power in reminding of something else	Aesthetic power in intrinsic attributes
Individualistic	Communal
Leaves us where it found us	Transforms sensibilities
Incapable of deep or sustained attention	Capable of repeated, careful attention
Lacks ambiguity	Allusive, suggests the transcendent
Tends toward relativism	Encourages understanding of others
Reflects the desires of self	Tends toward submission to standards

When traditional art forms are removed from us, we soon forget the impact they have had in our lives. As my son-in-law says, we remember stories, but we cannot remember why they moved us. Songs that used to evoke sincere emotion or inspiration in our hearts begin to blend with the static of our car radios. We laugh less and worry more. The grayness of the day becomes heavy and tedious, and still we hold on to the idea that something brighter awaits. I think of Dominguez High School in Compton, California, which mounted its first play in twenty years, without budget, stage, or trained students to form a cast. Two teachers undertook the daunting task of producing Thornton Wilder's *Our Town*, performed word-for-word but set in this violent Los Angeles suburb.

Dominguez students brought family photos of Mexican weddings and Catholic confirmations and funerals that were projected on screens placed on either side of a makeshift cafeteria platform during the play, which so eloquently discusses the meaningful rites of everyday life so often lost on us. The result was that this classic drama, set in a sleepy Midwestern town that had never heard of gang wars, came alive again in a crime-ridden Southern California community that wished to be known for more than drive-by shootings. With this production, the students reminded themselves and their audience that Compton was still "their town," the home of their births, courtships, marriages, christenings, and other celebrations.

I also think of hip-hop, trying again to retain its potential as a poetic and political force, before it was co-opted by the cultural machinery that rerouted its promise into more superficial and shabby fare. Obama's candidacy seemed to energize and mobilize the hip-hop community in a way that not much else could and to shape new possibilities for other forms of traditional culture. Maybe Maria Shriver is right. Maybe diversity in leadership, combined with a call to Americans to regard themselves once again as involved citizens rather than dazzled consumers, will reignite the original hope symbolized by California, and indeed, by all of America.

Examples abound. Across the California Southland and in numerous communities throughout the United States, a kind of renaissance may indeed be simmering. As in the medieval era, when local peasant groups began to crawl out from under the heavy hand of feudalism to establish townships and guilds with the aid of art festivals and cycle plays, Americans might yet disencumber themselves, through those same means, of the freeway systems and corporate chains that have smothered civic life and scattered neighborhoods. My fervent hope is that churches and universities will see a clear call to use their privileged position to facilitate these efforts. For several summers, my students have performed a "fractured" fairy tale for children at a local park (or even parking lot). A few years ago, they took up the story of *Sleeping Beauty* and related her experience to that of California. We too have fallen under a spell of sorts that has threatened to paralyze us and allow us to be overrun. But we are waking up.

Notes

Chapter 1 "Poppies, My Dear"

1. Stephen Schwartz, *From West to East: California and the Making of the American Mind* (New York: Free Press, 1988), 509.

2. Philip Cushman, "The Politics of Consumption," *Seattle Times*, October 19, 2004. Taken from Common Dreams News Center, www.commondreams.org/views04/1019-28.htm.

3. New York was and is called the Empire State, hence the Empire State Building.

Chapter 2 State Spirit

1. Eric Schlosser, *Fast Food Nation: The Dark Side of the All-American Meal* (Boston: Houghton Mifflin, 2001), 21.

2. Ibid., 37.

3. Ibid., 21.

4. Roger Lotchin, "The Triumphant Partnership: California Cities and the Winning of World War II," *Southern California Quarterly* 88, no. 1 (Spring 2006): 73.

5. Ibid., 72.

6. Ibid., 74.

7. Harry M. Benshoff and Sean Griffin, *America on Film: Representing Race, Class, Gender, and Sexuality at the Movies* (Oxford: Wiley-Blackwell, 2003), 181.

8. Traditional Fine Arts Organization Site Guide, Description of Pacific Arcadia Exhibition at Stanford University's Cantor Arts Center, 1999.

9. Walton Bean and James Rawls, *California: An Interpretive History* (Boston: McGraw-Hill, 2008), 52.

10. Father Pedro Font, personal communication.

11. Quoted in The History Channel's *In Search of History: Saints and Sinners of the California Missions*, DVD, directed by Mark Hufnail, written/coproduced by

Robert Gobeaux (A&E Television Networks, 1996). Marketed and distributed by New Video Group, New York.

12. Traditional Fine Arts Organization Site Guide, Description of Pacific Arcadia Exhibition at Stanford University's Cantor Arts Center, 1999.

13. Claire Perry, *Pacific Arcadia: Images of California, 1600–1915* (New York: Oxford University Press, 1999), 161.

14. www.tbn.org/index.php/3/10.html.

15. That line, according to Bennett Serf, actually was delivered to Moss Hart by Wolcott Gibbs. When Hart told Gibbs he'd had an oak tree on his Bucks County Estate moved in order to shade his library, Gibbs muttered, "It just goes to show you what God could do if he only had your money." Bennett Cerf, *Try and Stop Me: A Collection of Anecdotes and Stories, Mostly Humorous* (New York: Simon and Schuster, 1944), 27.

16. David Wyatt, *Five Fires: Race, Catastrophe, and the Shaping of California* (New York: Oxford University Press, 1997), 51.

17. Kevin Starr, "California—A Dream," in *California: A Place, A People, A Dream*, ed. Claudia K. Jurmain and James J. Rawls (San Francisco: Chronicle Books; Oakland: Oakland Museum, 1986), 16.

18. Thomas Andrews, "California History," Lecture, Azusa Pacific University, Azusa, CA., October 4, 2005.

19. Chuck Henry and Tara Wallis, "The New California Gold Rush: Modern-Day Gold Diggers Party Like It's 1849," *LA News*, www.nbclosangeles.com/news/local/NEW-CALIFORNIA-GOLD-RUSH.html. Geologists estimate that only about 20 percent of the gold in California was found during the gold rush, since most of it was buried so deeply in the mountains that it was simply unreachable with available technology. Mining in the Mother Lode is still a laborious and dicey task, even with modern equipment.

Chapter 3 The Rest Is Mystery

1. Andrew Rolle, *California: A History*, 5th ed. (Wheeling, IL: Harlan Davidson, 1998), 1.

2. Kevin Starr, *California: A History* (New York: Modern Library, 2005), 5.

3. Montalvo, quoted in Starr, *California: A History*, 5.

4. Ibid., 6.

5. Ibid.

6. Walt Disney, "True Life Fantasy," *E-Ticket*, Fall 2005, 3.

7. Ibid.

8. G. K. Chesterton, *Orthodoxy* (New York: Doubleday, 2001), 51, 62.

9. Umberto Eco, *Travels in Hyperreality: Essays*, trans. W. Weaver (New York: Harcourt Brace Jovanovich, 1986), 46.

10. Denise Chavez, "My Long Hot Ramona Summer," introduction to Helen Hunt Jackson, *Ramona* (New York: Modern Library Classics, 2005), xiii.

11. This is taken from Thomas Andrews, who teaches California History at Azusa Pacific University and helped appropriate the school's Special Collection of California Literature. Tom was formerly executive director of the Historical Society of Southern California.

12. David Wyatt, *Five Fires: Race, Catastrophe, and the Shaping of California* (New York: Oxford University Press, 1997), 70–71.

13. Ibid., 106.

14. Stanley Hauerwas, *After Christendom? How the Church Is to Behave if Freedom, Justice, and a Christian Nation Are Bad Ideas* (Nashville: Abingdon, 1991), 9.

15. Walter Brueggemann, *The Prophetic Imagination* (Minneapolis: Fortress, 2001), 1–2.

16. Michael Billig, *Freudian Repression: Conversation Creating the Unconscious* (Cambridge: Cambridge University Press, 1999), 141. As Gustavo Gutiérrez writes, "Power held in the present tends to make provision for the future as well, by dominating the past of the vanquished. A people afflicted with amnesia are an unstable people, subservient to the idols of the status quo, vulnerable to the self-serving, mendacious word. Conquerors always try to erase or block the memory of those whose necks they have bent." Gustavo Gutiérrez, *Las Casas: In Search of the Poor of Jesus Christ* (Maryknoll, NY: Orbis Books, 1993), 413.

17. Rollo May, *The Cry for Myth* (New York: W. W. Norton, 1991), 103.

18. Herbert Marcuse, *Eros and Civilization* (Boston: Beacon, 1974).

19. Ibid., 55.

20. Wyatt, *Five Fires*, 116–17.

21. Ibid., 110.

22. Ibid., 119.

23. Brian Fagan, *Snapshots of the Past* (Walnut Creek, CA: AltaMira, 1995), 157.

24. Wyatt, *Five Fires*, 155.

25. Ibid., 134.

26. Stuart Ewen and Elizabeth Ewen, *Channels of Desire: Mass Images and the Shaping of American Consciousness* (New York: McGraw-Hill, 1982).

27. Svetlana Boym, *The Future of Nostalgia* (New York: Basic Books, 2001), 35.

28. Bryce McNeil, "Marrying Decade Nostalgia with Nostalgia for the Present: The Transformation of VH1," Paper presentation, annual convention of the Southwest Texas Popular & American Culture Association Conference, Albuquerque, New Mexico, February 14–17, 2007, 3.

29. Ibid., 8.

30. Eric Foner and John Sayles, "Movies and History," in *Media Journal: Reading and Writing about Popular Culture*, ed. Joseph Harris, Jay Rosen, and Gary Calpas (Boston: Allyn and Bacon, 1999).

31. Robert Scholes, Nancy R. Comley, Carl H. Klaus, and Michael Silverman, *Elements of Literature* (New York: Oxford University Press, 1991), 122.

32. Alasdair MacIntyre, *After Virtue: A Study in Moral Theory* (Notre Dame, IN: University of Notre Dame Press, 1981), 201.

33. W. R. Fisher, "Narration as a Human Communication Paradigm: The Case of Public Moral Argument," *Communication Monographs* 51 (1984): 15.

34. Ibid., 12.

35. G. Braxton and R. W. Welkos, "The Death of Reality," *Los Angeles Times*, December 13, 1992.

36. Ibid., 7.

37. S. Mitchell, "Stone, Writers Debate 'JKF' Fact, Fiction," *Los Angeles Times*, March 5, 1992.

38. Ibid.

39. Norman M. Klein, *The History of Forgetting: Los Angeles and the Erasure of Memory* (London: Verso, 1998).

40. Alan Nadel, *Flatlining in the Field of Dreams: Cultural Narratives in the Films of President Reagan's America* (New Brunswick, NJ: Rutgers University Press, 1997).

41. Full text of speech delivered at 2004 Republican Convention, www.usatoday.com/news/politicselections/nation/president/2004-08-31-schwarzeneggerfulltext_x.htm.

42. Eco, *Travels in Hyperreality*, 14.

43. Oscar Brockett, *History of the Theatre* (Boston: Allyn and Bacon, 1999), 493.

44. Frank J. Barrett and Suresh Srivastva, "History as a Mode of Inquiry in Organizational Life: A Role for Human Cosmogony," *Human Relations* 44 (1991): 252.

45. Jacques Ellul, *Propaganda: The Formation of Men's Attitudes* (1965; repr., New York: Vintage Books, 1973).

46. www.cornerstonetheater.org/content/index.php?option=com_content&view=article&id=15&Itemid=46.

47. In 2007, Stephen Colbert's manufactured word, *truthiness*, was named the "Word of the Year," and it now enjoys definitions in Webster's Dictionary: (1) "Truth that comes from the gut, not books"; (2) "The quality of preferring concepts or facts one wishes to be true, rather than concepts or facts known to be true" (www.merriam-webster.com/info/06words.htm). Truthiness is the result of historical amnesia and will work to benefit the powerful and oppress the rest. Such phenomena always have.

Chapter 4 Extreme Reality

1. Quentin Schultze discusses this point at length in *Christianity and the Mass Media in America: Toward a Democratic Accommodation* (East Lansing, MI: Michigan State University Press, 2003).

2. Richard Campbell, *Media and Culture: An Introduction to Mass Communication* (New York: St. Martin's Press, 2002) 186–88. For current statistics concerning the state of television viewing, please consult Norman Herr's "Television and Health," www.csun.edu/science/health/docs/tv&health.html.

3. John Carman, "TV So Bad That It's Classic," *Los Angeles Times*, February 2, 1995, E1.

4. Howard Blake, "The Worst Program in TV History," in *TV Book: The Ultimate Television Book*, ed. Judy Fireman (New York: Workman, 1977), 96.

5. Walter Fisher argues that stories are used to make sense of life and to create moral arguments in "Narration as a Human Communication Paradigm: The Case of Public Moral Argument," *Communication Monographs* 51 (1984): 1–22.

6. Dominant culture occasionally selects token individuals from potentially troublesome subcultures for special treatment while returning the rest to society's margins, creating a false sense of fair play, equal participation in "the pursuit of happiness," and the possibility that one can succeed if one tries hard enough and/or "has what it takes," according to Jonathan Kamin, "Taking the Roll Out of Rock and Roll: Reverse Acculturation," *Popular Music and Society* 3 (1972): 10–15.

7. Blake, "The Worst Program in TV History," 96–100.

8. Karen E. Rowe, "Feminism and Fairy Tales," in *Don't Bet on the Prince: Contemporary Feminist Fairy Tales in North America and England*, ed. Jack Zipes (New York: Routledge, 1986), 217.

9. Ibid.

10. Hazel Henderson, "Eco-Feminism and Eco-Communication: Toward the Feminization of Economics," in *Communications at the Crossroads: The Gender Gap Connection*, ed. Ramona Rush and Donna Allen (Norwood, NJ: Ablex, 1989), 289–303.

11. Stuart Ewen and Elizabeth Ewen, *Channels of Desire: Mass Images and the Shaping of American Consciousness* (New York: McGraw-Hill, 1982), 47.

12. Ibid., 265.

13. Something about the failure of traditional cultural modes and the unraveling of customary human bonds made people particularly receptive to the lure of "the new." As mass advertising made "familiarity out of spectacle, the dull familiarities of daily life were now confronted by the dazzling familiarity of promise" (ibid., 57–62).

14. Todd Gitlin, "Prime Time Ideology," *Social Problems* 26, no. 3 (February 1979): 513. "Advertising is engineered social order . . . organizing masses of strangers into reliable, national markets of consumers," according to Ronald Berman, "Advertising and Social Change in Twentieth Century Advertising and the Economy of Abundance," *Advertising Age*, Special Issue, April 30, 1980, 8.

15. Ewen and Ewen, *Channels of Desire*, 47–53.

16. Bennett Cerf, *Try and Stop Me: A Collection of Anecdotes and Stories, Mostly Humorous* (New York: Simon and Schuster, 1944), 27.

17. J. R. Dolan, *The Yankee Peddlers of Early America* (New York: Bramhall House, 1964).

18. Gitlin, "Prime Time Ideology," 513–15.

19. Ann Swidler, "Culture in Action: Symbols and Strategies," *American Sociological Review* 51 (April 1986): 273–86. According to Swidler, ritual acquires added significance in unsettled lives. "People developing new strategies of action depend on cultural models to learn styles of self, relationship, cooperation, authority and so forth" (279). During such times people's actions are not determined by taken-for-granted value systems, but by the "available choices" seen within a culture (281). These choices will eventually create new values, which become more tacit during settled times and more determinative of people's actions.

20. Ibid., 284.

21. Ewen and Ewen, *Channels of Desire*, 93.

22. Judith Williamson argues that the symbolic value of women in American mass culture actually might outweigh their considerable economic value. Judith Williamson, "Woman Is an Island: Femininity and Colonization," in *Studies in Entertainment: Critical Approaches to Mass Culture*, ed. Tania Modleski (Bloomington, IN: Indiana University Press, 1986), 97–117. Women, the guardians of "personal life," become a kind of dumping ground for all the values society wants off its back but must be perceived to cherish. It is as if Western capitalism can hold up an image of freedom and fulfillment and say, "Look, our system offers this!" while in fact the reason these values are squeezed into personal life (and a tight squeeze it is, too) is that they are exactly what the economic system fundamentally negates, based as it is on the values of competition and profit, producing lack of control, lack of choice, and alienation (106).

23. Clive James, *Fame in the Twentieth Century* (New York: Random House, 1993), 131.

24. Ibid.

25. Ibid., 134.

26. "Americans have a unique hunger to identify with personalities, larger-than-life personalities especially. No country in the world is as driven by personality as this one," observes David Shaw in "Hunger for Heroes, Villains, Rooted in American Psyche," *Los Angeles Times*, February 17, 1994, G7.

27. Essentially, "an appearance on . . . television . . . is the ultimate certification of 'making it' in America . . . simply to gain recognition, to prove, merely by showing up, that [one is] 'somebody,'" writes Donna Woolfolk Cross, *Mediaspeak: How Television Makes Up Your Mind* (New York: Coward-McCann, 1983), 148.

28. David Brooks, *Bobos in Paradise: The New Upper Class and How They Got There* (New York: Simon and Schuster, 2000).

Chapter 5 Who Is My Neighbor?

1. David Wyatt, *Five Fires: Race, Catastrophe, and the Shaping of California* (New York: Oxford University Press, 1997), 61.

2. Claire Perry, *Pacific Arcadia: Images of California, 1600–1915* (New York: Oxford University Press, 1999), 182.

3. Ibid., 239.

4. Ibid., 87.

5. Ibid.

6. Ibid., 2.

7. Wyatt, *Five Fires*, 74–75.

8. Ibid.

9. Ibid., 86.

10. Ibid., 158.

11. Ibid.

12. Ibid., 193.

13. Chester Himes, *If He Hollers Let Him Go: A Novel* (New York: Thunder's Mouth, 1986), 73.

14. Ibid., 159.

15. Wyatt, *Five Fires*, 211.

16. Neil Postman, *Technopoly: The Surrender of Culture to Technology* (New York: Vintage, 1989), 89–90.

17. Maureen Rans, "New Survivor Color Coordinated," *Monterey County Herald*, August 25, 1996, D1.

18. Wyatt, *Five Fires*, 116.

19. Perry, *Pacific Arcadia*, 136.

20. Ibid.

21. Ibid.

22. Ibid.

23. Ibid.

24. Wyatt, *Five Fires*, 153.

25. Ibid., 154.

26. Ibid., 215.

27. *Exploring the Avant-garde*, VHS, directed by Peter Sellars (Princeton, NJ: Films for the Humanities & Sciences, 2003).

28. Ray Oldenburg has written extensively about the lack of a "Third Place" in current culture. If the First Place is the home and the Second Place is our place of

work or school, the Third Place would be a public hangout of some kind, such as the town square used to provide a place for us to converse with our neighbors. See Ray Oldenburg, *The Great Good Place: Cafés, Coffee Shops, Bookstores, Bars, Hair Salons and Other Hangouts at the Heart of a Community* (New York: Marlowe & Company, 1999).

29. Luke 19:10 reads, "The Son of Man came to seek and to save what was lost" (NIV).

30. Henry Louis Gates Jr., discussing the police profiling of black men, observes, "There's a moving violation that many African Americans know as DWB, Driving While Black." See "Thirteen Ways of Looking at a Black Man," in *Media Journal: Reading and Writing about Popular Culture*, Joseph Harris, Jay Rosen, and Gary Calpas (Boston: Allyn and Bacon, 1999), 164.

31. Benjamin DeMott argues that race problems are nearly always represented in popular media as being personal problems rather than systemic ones. See "Visions of Black–White Friendship," in Harris, Rosen, and Calpas, *Media Journal*, 90–103.

32. Christine Pohl, "The Modern Challenges to the Practice of Hospitality," *Mars Hill Audio Journal* 41 (1999).

Chapter 6 The Mastered Race

1. Tournament of Roses, Telecast Director: Stephanie Medina, Executive Producer: Joe Quasarano, KTLA Studios, Los Angeles, CA, January 1, 2005.

2. Richard Keyes, "The Idol Factory," in *No God but God: Breaking with the Idols of Our Age*, ed. Os Guinness and J. Seel (Chicago: Moody, 1992), 29–48.

3. David Bordwell, Janet Staiger, and Kristin Thompson, *The Classical Hollywood Cinema: Film Style and Mode of Production to 1960* (New York: Columbia University Press, 1985).

4. Craig Detweiler and Barry Taylor, *A Matrix of Meanings: Finding God in Pop Culture* (Grand Rapids: Baker Academic, 2003).

5. Peter Brooks, *The Melodramatic Imagination: Balzac, Henry James, Melodrama, and the Mode of Excess* (New Haven, CT: Yale University Press, 1976), 20–22.

6. *How Art Made the World*. BBC Documentary: British Broadcasting Company, 2006.

7. Companies cannot actually own genes, but they can own the process by which they are extrapolated. See *Genetic Engineering and Biotechnology News* for current news on what it calls "BioBusiness, " www.genengnews.com/biobusiness.

8. Jeremy Rifkin, "The Biotech Century: Harnessing the Gene and Remaking the World," *Mars Hill Audio Journal* 34 (1998).

9. Miriam Piven Cotler, *AARP Bulletin* 46, No. 7 (2005): 13.

10. Ibid.

11. Dorothy L. Sayers, "Vocation in Work," in *A Christian Basis for the Post-War World*, ed. A. E. Baker (New York: Morehouse-Gorham, 1942), 89–90. A footnote on p. 89 says that this talk was abridged from an address delivered at The Dome, Brighton, on March 8, 1941.

12. Ibid., 91.

13. *Who Needs Sleep?* directed by Haskell Wexler and Lisa Leeman (United States, 2005).

14. John Caughey, "Imaginary Social Relationships," in *Media Journal: Reading and Writing about Popular Culture*, ed. Joseph Harris, Jay Rosen, and Gary Calpas (Boston: Allyn and Bacon, 1999), 45–69.

15. Bruce Miller, *The Actor as Storyteller* (Mountain View, CA: Mayfield 2000).

16. Joan Acocella, "Out of Character," *The New Yorker*, March 3, 2003, 42.

17. www.femalefirst.co.uk/celebrity/Jessica+Simpson-8945.html.

18. Gene Edward Veith, *God at Work* (Wheaton: Crossway Books, 2002).

19. www.scientology.org.

20. James A. Herrick, "Science, Science Fiction, and Spirituality: Inventing the Post-Christian West's New Religion" (speech delivered at Westminster Seminary, Escondido, CA, 2005). The ideas behind that formal presentation resulted in the book by Herrick, *Scientific Mythologies: How Science and Science Fiction Forge New Religious Beliefs* (Downer's Grove, IL: InterVarsity, 2008).

21. "Playboy Interview: Stanley Kubrick," in *The Making of 2001: A Space Odyssey*, ed. Stephanie Schwam (New York: Modern Library, 2000), 274.

22. Herrick, "Science, Science Fiction, and Spirituality."

23. www.scientology.org.

24. www.prohelpgroup.com/free_personality_test.html and www.rehabilitatenz.co.nz/pages/stress-test-info.html

25. www.scientology.cc/articles/603292245311.vm.

26. www.scientologyreligion.org/pg006.html.

27. www.scientology.org/religion/presentation/pg009.html.

28. www.scientology.org/religion/presentation/pg014.html.

29. Hebrews 11:6 (NIV).

30. www.scientology-newyork.org/scientology/index.html.

31. Herrick, "Science, Science Fiction, and Spirituality."

32. *Esalen Catalogue*, September 2004.

33. Herrick, "Science, Science Fiction, and Spirituality."

34. Brett Wilbur, "Making Room," *Monterey Country Weekly*, February 24–March 2, 2005, 17–19.

35. Barbara Ehrenreich, *Nickel and Dimed: On (Not) Getting By in America* (New York: Holt, 2002), 69.

36. Herrick "Science, Science Fiction, and Spirituality."

Chapter 7 Sunshiny Mournings

1. Evelyn Waugh, *The Loved One: An Anglo-American Tragedy* (Boston: Little, Brown and Company, 1948), 47.

2. Ibid., 49.

3. Ibid., 48.

4. Ibid., 112.

5. Ibid., 43.

6. Ibid., 78.

7. Ibid., 46.

8. Ibid., 62.

9. Ibid., 141.

10. Ibid., 122–23.

11. Walter Brueggemann, *The Prophetic Imagination* (Minneapolis: Fortress, 2001), 1–2.

12. www.hollywoodforever.com.

13. John Cloud, "Metting Your (Film) Maker," *Time Magazine Special Issue*, July 10, 2000, www.time.com/time/reports/mississippi/cassity.html.

14. Bill McKibben, *The Age of Missing Information* (New York: Random House, 1992), 147.

15. Frank Rich, "What O. J. Passed to the Gipper," *New York Times*, June 20, 2004, www.nytimes.com/2004/06/20/arts/what-o-j-passed-to-the-gipper.html?sec=&spon=&pagewanted=1.

16. Ibid.

17. Ibid.

18. Brueggemann, *Prophetic Imagination*, 88.

19. Ibid., 11.

20. www.americanrhetoric.com/speeches/alexandersolzhenitsynharvard.htm.

21. Brueggemann, *Prophetic Imagination*, 56.

22. Ibid., 56–57.

23. G. K. Chesterton, *Orthodoxy* (New York: Doubleday, 2001), 52, 56.

24. www.arlingtonwestsantamonica.org.

25. Brueggemann, *Prophetic Imagination*, 90.

26. Ibid., 91.

Chapter 8 'Til Death Do Us Part, or Whatever

1. www.theweddingreport.com.

2. Deborah Hornblow, "The States of Marriage: In Pursuit of the Perfect Union, a Nation Comes Up Empty (Or Divorced)," *The Detroit News*, March 15, 2003, D1.

3. WWD Staff, "Suzy," *Women's Wear Daily*, April 15, 2003, www.wwd.com/lifestyle-news/eye/suzy-734470.

4. Phillip Vannini, "Will You Marry Me? Spectacle and Consumption in the Ritual of Marriage Proposals," *Journal of Popular Culture* 38 (2004): 170.

5. Ibid., 171.

6. Ibid., 174.

7. Ibid., 183.

8. Evelyn Waugh, *The Loved One: An Anglo-American Tragedy* (Boston: Little, Brown and Company, 1948), 106.

9. Ibid., 134–35.

10. Naomi Wolf, *The Beauty Myth: How Images of Beauty Are Used against Women* (New York: Morrow, 1991), 17.

11. Ibid., 64.

12. Betty Friedan, "The Sexual Sell," in *The Feminine Mystique* (Harmondsworth: Penguin Books, 1982), 208–10.

13. Wolf, *Beauty Myth*, 65.

14. Ibid., 85.

15. Ibid., 17.

16. Marjorie Rosen, *Popcorn Venus: Women, Movies, and the American Dream* (New York: Coward, McMann and Geoghegan, 1973).

17. Barbara Ehrenreich, "Playboy Joins the Battle of the Sexes," in *Media Journal: Reading and Writing about Popular Culture*, ed. Joseph Harris, Jay Rosen, and Gary Calpas (Boston: Allyn and Bacon, 1999), 105–11.

18. Julie Jeffrey, *Frontier Women: The Trans-Mississippi West, 1840–1880* (New York: Hill and Wang, 1979), 120.

19. Stanley Cavell, *Pursuits of Happiness: The Hollywood Comedy of Remarriage* (Cambridge, MA: Harvard University Press, 1984), 27.

20. Ibid., 61.

21. Ibid., 64.

22. Robert N. Bellah, *Habits of the Heart: Individualism and Commitment in American Life* (Berkeley: University of California Press, 1985), 264.

23. J. S. Holliday, William Swain, and Howard Roberts Lamar, *The World Rushed In: The California Gold Rush Experience* (New York: Simon & Schuster, 1981), 369.

24. J. H. Carson, "Early Recollections of the Mines," *San Joaquin Republican*, 1852.

25. Eric Schlosser, *Fast Food Nation: The Dark Side of the All-American Meal* (Boston: Houghton Mifflin, 2001), 43.

26. David Wyatt, *Five Fires: Race, Catastrophe, and the Shaping of California* (New York: Oxford University Press, 1997), 180.

27. Bill Moyers, *A Mind for Music with Peter Sellars* (PBS Video, 1990).

28. Bill McKibben, *The Age of Missing Information* (New York: Random House, 1992), 143–44.

29. Peter H. Burnett, *Recollections and Opinions of an Old Pioneer* (New York: Da Capo, 1969), 301.

Chapter 9 The Golden Chariot

1. Raymond Williams would ask who are these masses, anyway, these nameless strangers, these "other people"? What are their aspirations and struggles and how are these pacified through cultural institutions? He notes an intricate relationship between *popular/folk culture*, stemming from the everyday lives of real people, and *popular/mass culture* or *commodity culture*, which seeks to represent and reproduce everyday life for profit. At the Rendezvous, we see the dynamics of a so-called popular (commodity) culture that is not popularly produced, but is rather the product of "professionals who share nothing of the lives that they are reproducing," professionals who "learn to produce an extraordinary idiomatic facsimile of those lives." One essential dynamic seems to involve the exploitation and appropriation of "real needs that [the commodity culture industry] has clearly engaged, even though . . . it has falsified and alienated them." The Route 66 "Rendezvous" seems to meet the needs and fulfill the dreams of everyday people in a community setting.

Stephen Heath and Gillian Skirrow, transcript of a videotaped interview with Raymond Williams prepared for the conference on Mass Culture, Center for Twentieth Century Studies, and published as *Studies in Entertainment: Critical Approaches to Mass Culture*, ed. Tania Modleski (Bloomington, IN: Indiana University Press, 1986), 7–8.

2. Purchasing a car may be the last "great hunt" for young men coming of age in California.

3. As mentioned in previous chapters, the postwar decades of the hot rod and muscle car were turbulent and unsettled. According to Ann Swidler, ritual acquires added significance in unsettled lives. "People developing new strategies of action depend on cultural models to learn styles of self, relationship, cooperation, authority and so forth." Ann Swidler, "Culture in Action: Symbols and Strategies," *American Sociological Review* 51 (1986): 279.

4. Arthur M. Okun, *Equality and Efficiency: The Big Tradeoff* (Washington, DC: Brookings Institution, 1975).

5. Umberto Eco, *Travels in Hyperreality: Essays*, trans. W. Weaver (New York: Harcourt Brace Jovanovich, 1986), 48.

6. Dave Hickey, *Air Guitar: Essays on Art and Democracy* (Los Angeles: Art Issues Press, 1997), 69.

7. Ibid., 70.

8. Ibid.

9. Ibid., 68.

10. Rollo May, *The Cry for Myth* (New York: W. W. Norton, 1991), 88–89.

11. Hickey, *Air Guitar*, 67.

12. Ibid., 66.

13. Ibid., 67.

14. The DeLorean and other famous "movie autos" were on display at the Los Angeles Fair a couple of years ago. They drew quite a crowd.

15. Mircea Eliade, *The Sacred and the Profane: The Nature of Religion* (Orlando, FL: Harcourt-Brace, 1959), 68.

16. Ibid. Eliade further notes that when we mass produce, we become godlike, we make the old new, we unleash abundance.

17. Ibid., 101.

18. Ibid., 88.

19. Ibid., 92.

20. Ibid., 88.

Chapter 10 East of Eating

1. Carl Sagan's view was that in our human evolution, we could go from planet to planet, happily consuming the resources represented in the vast smorgasbord of space: "a million little worlds in the Oort Comet cloud," for starters. Carl Sagan, *Pale Blue Dot: A Vision of the Human Future in Space* (New York: Random House, 1994), 387.

Like Sagan, the branch of church concentrating on its rapture to the heavens need have little concern for the future of this planet. The only problem is that God has told us to take care of the earth, and in less nonchalant terms than a parent telling their spoiled children to take care of their toys when all the time the children know there are plenty more where those came from. Moreover, Christ has asked that when he returns, we should be busily loving our neighbor, not pillaging their land and robbing them of their livelihood.

2. For the history of the South Central Los Angeles Farm, see Mike Boehm, "Theater: Cornerstone Mobilizes the Troupe: The Normally Slow and Steady Theater Company Takes to the Streets over the South Central Farm Eviction. A New Leaf?" *Los Angeles Times*, June 25, 2006; Erika Hayasaki, "Seeds of Dissension Linger: Farmers in the South Central Community Decry the Loss of the Land to a Warehouse Project,"

Los Angeles Times, October 31, 2005; Daniel Hernandez, "Bushel of Complaints," *L.A. Weekly*, March 17, 2006; Daniel Hernandez, "A Brown Day in L.A.: Mayor V. Faces Global Immigration Issues—and Angry Farmers," *L.A. Weekly*, May 25, 2006; Daniel Hernandez and David Zahniser, "Seeds of Secrecy," *L.A. Weekly*, March 10, 2006; Bill Hetherman, "Attorney: City Sold South Central Farm at Major Loss for Taxpayers," *City News Service*, July 13, 2006; Jessica Hoffmann, "History of the South Central Farm: How the Community Has Used the Land Since 1985," *New Standard*, April 5, 2006; Brent Hopkins, "The End for South Central Farm?" *Daily News of Los Angeles*, June 14, 2006; Brent Hopkins, "Last Gasp in Fight for Farm: 10 Arrested as Activists Attempt to Stop Bulldozer," *Daily News of Los Angeles*, July 6, 2006; Connie Llanos, "Judge Rules on Urban Garden: Sale to Developer Is Upheld," *Daily News of Los Angeles*, July 27, 2006; Art Marroquin, "Deputies Evict Farmers, Supporters from South Central Farm," *City News Service*, June 13, 2006; Brenda Norrell, "Navajo Says Evictions of Farmers from Urban Farm Sends a Message," *Indian Country Today*, June 21, 2006; Emanuel Parker, "Huntington Housing Ex-farm's Trees," *Pasadena-Star News*, December 15, 2006. Research sources courtesy of Craig Keen, Azusa Pacific University.

3. David Wyatt, *Five Fires: Race, Catastrophe, and the Shaping of California* (New York: Oxford University Press, 1997), 13.

4. My colleague, Craig Keen, from Azusa Pacific University's Theology Department, has written beautifully and extensively about the South Central Farm. This is taken from a chapter manuscript of his upcoming book with the working title *Working Out the Body and Blood of Christ on the Eighth Day of Creation: Toward a Martyr-Ecclesiology*.

5. Rufina Juarez, interview by Craig Keen, August 1, 2006.

6. This opening of "the Alameda Corridor" meant that property along Alameda Avenue would become once more very valuable. "The Alameda Corridor" runs immediately across the street from South Central Farm. It is hard to believe that anyone would have wanted to spend good "development" money for the Farm when it fell into the hands of South Central LA residents just after the 1992 riots. See the Alameda Corridor Transportation Authority website, www.acta.org (accessed June 12, 2007): "The Alameda Corridor is a 20-mile-long rail cargo expressway linking the ports of Long Beach and Los Angeles to the transcontinental rail network near downtown Los Angeles. It is a series of bridges, underpasses, overpasses and street improvements that separate freight trains from street traffic and passenger trains, facilitating a more efficient transportation network. The project's centerpiece is the Mid-Corridor Trench, which will carry freight trains in an open trench that is 10 miles long, 33 feet deep and 50 feet wide between State Route 91 in Carson and 25th Street in Los Angeles. Construction began in April 1997. Operations began in April 2002." Courtesy of Craig Keen.

7. Taken from Craig Keen's manuscript *Working Out the Body and Blood of Christ on the Eighth Day of Creation*, 5.

8. What seemed to make this battle newsworthy for most was the farm's support from various celebrities, perhaps most notably that of Daryl Hannah, who occupied a tree overnight and physically joined the struggle against eviction.

9. Glen Gendzel, "Not Just a Golden State: Three Anglo 'Rushes' in the Making of Southern California, 1880–1920," *Southern California Quarterly* 90, no. 4 (Winter 2008–2009): 366.

10. Ibid., 366–67.

11. Ibid., 368.

12. Ibid., 370.

13. Ibid., 370–71.

14. Taken from Craig Keen's manuscript *Working Out the Body and Blood of Christ on the Eighth Day of Creation*, 5.

15. John Steinbeck, *The Grapes of Wrath* (New York: Penguin, 1992), 315.

16. Ibid.

17. Ibid., 316.

18. Ibid., 318–19.

19. Proverbs 13:23 (NIV).

20. Eric Schlosser, *Fast Food Nation: The Dark Side of the All-American Meal* (Boston: Houghton Mifflin, 2001), 3.

21. Ibid., 83.

22. Philippians 3:19 (NIV).

23. Sallie Tisdale, "A Weight That Women Carry," in *Media Journal: Reading and Writing about Popular Culture*, ed. Joseph Harris, Jay Rosen, and Gary Calpas (Boston: Allyn and Bacon, 1999), 466.

24. Jean Kilbourne, "Slim Hopes: Advertising and the Obsession with Thinness," video produced and directed by Sut Jhally (Mediated Education Foundation, 1995).

25. Rudolph Bell, *Holy Anorexia* (Chicago: University of Chicago Press, 1985), 52–53.

26. Schlosser, *Fast Food Nation*, 123.

27. Ibid., 122.

28. John Thorne, "The Machine in the Kitchen," in Harris, Rosen, and Calpas, *Media Journal*, 460.

29. Ibid.

30. Wyatt, *Five Fires*, 14.

31. Acts 14:17.

32. Robert Farrar Capon, *The Supper of the Lamb: A Culinary Reflection* (New York: Modern Library, 2002), 40.

33. G. K. Chesterton, *Orthodoxy* (New York: Doubleday, 2001), 48–51.

34. Sarah Covin Juengst, *Breaking Bread: The Spiritual Significance of Food* (Louisville: Westminster John Knox, 1992), 50.

Chapter 11 Choosing Life

1. www.youtube.com/watch?v=62_ajoKkuHA.

2. John Steinbeck, *East of Eden* (New York: Penguin, 2002), 262.

3. Ibid., 301.

4. Ibid., 268.

5. Ibid., 411.

6. W. R. Fisher, "Narration as a Human Communication Paradigm: The Case of Public Moral Argument," *Communication Monographs* 51 (1984): 1–22.

7. Richard Campbell, *Media and Culture: An Introduction to Mass Communication* (New York: St. Martin's Press, 1998).

8. Kenneth A. Myers, *All God's Children and Blue Suede Shoes: Christians and Popular Culture* (Wheaton: Good News, 1989), 120.